# Stress Control

Vernon Coleman is the author of *The Medicine Men, Paper Doctors, Everything you want to know about ageing,* and *Stress Control.*
He also writes 'funny' books, and two weekly columns, one of which is syndicated to the newspapers around the world. He is a fellow of the Royal Society of Medicine.

Dr Coleman relieves his stress by watching cricket, and adds to it by buying books faster than anyone could possibly read them. Born in 1946, he is married with two children and fifteen apple trees, and has been a general practitioner for six years.

Vernon Coleman

# Stress Control

**Pan Books** London and Sydney

**Acknowledgements** I should like to thank Peggy who looked after my physical and mental wellbeing, my literary agent Anne McDermid of David Higham Associates, and Eileen Reynolds who produced the typescript efficiently and with a never-failing smile.

First published in Great Britain 1978 by Maurice Temple Smith Ltd.
This edition published 1980 by Pan Books Ltd,
Cavaye Place, London SW10 9PG
© 1978 Vernon Coleman
ISBN 0 330 25914 8
Printed and bound in Great Britain by
Cox & Wyman Ltd, Reading

# Contents

Preface 1

**Part one:**
**Stresses and strains, pressures and pains** 3
Introduction 4
Environmental pressures 7
Sources of social strains 17
Personal pains 25

**Part two:**
**The counterstress philosophy** 33
Introduction 34
The early warning signs 35
Identify the factors which cause stress 36
Your counterstress checklist 37
Know yourself 41
How do you cope with problems? 43
The four cornerstones of life 50
The values and limitations of medical intervention 55
Stress-proof your body 63
Learning to relax 89
Summary: the counterstress philosophy in brief 116

**Part three:**
**The diseases caused by stress** 111
Introduction 112
Symptoms and causes 114

**Appendix:**
**The mechanism of stress** 203
Introduction 204

# Preface

Staying alive and healthy today is like staying alive and healthy in the middle of a war. The ever-present enemy is not armed with tanks or machine guns, and kills and maims not with bullets but with stress.

Before you can defend yourself you need information about the enemy. Success in any battle depends upon knowing what the enemy is planning and what he is likely to do. To survive and stay healthy you must learn to recognize the problems and pressures which affect you. Once identified the enemy can often be avoided. This is the subject of Part One of this book.

Preparing the defences is the subject of Part Two. In order to minimise the damage inflicted by the enemy's attacks you must improve your physical and mental strength. In addition there are quite a few tricks you can acquire to help you ward off the enemy's challenges.

However good the defences are there will be unforeseen casualties in any war. It helps if you can spot signs of breeches developing in your defences as soon as possible. It also helps if you know what to do when wounds are sustained and you need first aid or professional attention. Part Three of the book will help you here. If you want to look up particular symptoms or problems that are troubling you, there is a list on pages 114-116.

VC 1978

# Part One
## Stresses and Strains, Pressures and Pains

This part of the book deals with the causes of stress.
These are divided into three main groups: environmental,
social and personal.

## AN INTRODUCTION

In order to cope with and prevent stress diseases it is necessary to know what *causes* stress.

It is not possible to make a comprehensive list of all the possible pressures and strains to which human beings are likely to find themselves subjected (although the accompanying table lists some obvious causes of stress). We are all constantly under siege and anything, deliberately sought or accidentally found, pleasant or unpleasant, that increases the intensity of life causes an increase, temporary or permanent, in the pressure of living. Changes in the external environment and changes in the mental or emotional outlook of the individual are equally likely to produce distress. There are the ordinary daily tensions such as those produced by the car breaking down. There are development crises which we all go through when we start school or leave home. And there are the crises in our life when we are threatened by serious illness or when we take the plunge and get married or buy our first house.

Many strains are produced at home. Getting married, separated or divorced all produce pressure as do coping with the death of a close friend or relative. Injury and illness, pregnancy, rows with relatives and moving home all add to the strains we bear. At work a change in the level of responsibility, a change in job specifications, getting fired or being forced to retire all produce pressure. Court cases, going on holiday, leaving college and filing for bankruptcy are other obvious causes of strain. Uncertainty is one of the major causes of distress. While waiting for the examination results to be posted or for the court to return with its verdict we suffer more than we do when the worst is known. Suspense is a genuine killer.

Research published in the *Journal of Psychomatic Research* in 1967 showed that alterations in life style can be dangerous. When three thousand sailors and marines were studied it was found that a cluster of important changes in a pattern of living often preceded either one illness or a collection of illnesses. Major changes in life (such as marriage, the death of a close relative or a change of employment) often preceded a major

4

illness. The death of a marital partner, exposure to personal danger and other important crises often preceded a collapse. An article in the *Lancet* in 1963 showed that widows and widowers die much younger than others with comparable medical histories. Widowhood seems to accelerate ageing in young people. It is even established that good news can be fatal. Triumph as well as grief, rage and fear can induce a heart attack or a stroke. Patients with heart disease have been reported by Dr Engel of the University of Rochester School of Medicine to have died on being reunited with relatives after a long separation, and on holding a royal straight flush in a poker game. One man even died while celebrating his doctor's verdict that his heart was sound.

Many strains and pressures are sought, of course. Pleasant experiences, although often short-lived and unlikely to lead to major emotional problems, produce stress reactions within the body. Researchers have shown that when enjoying comedy films, exciting television programmes, erotic experiences or success at work, our body reacts in exactly the same way that it would react if we were to be faced with unwelcome experiences. And the changes produced may be an asset as well as a disadvantage. Many journalists claim that they work better when their deadline is dangerously close: the pressure caused by the lack of time available helps them produce their best work.

Inevitably, the *effect* the strain has on any individual depends upon a number of other factors. Age, health and intelligence are important but social standing, past experiences and learned values are also relevant. For example, when old and weak, we are less capable of coping with problems and the more intelligent a man the greater the chances of his suffering badly when under unavoidable pressure. The effect a potential stressor has on the body also depends on the attitude of the victim. Bing Crosby only ever showed tension while playing golf; he took it very seriously and died of a heart attack on a golf course in Spain.

People who are under continual pressure will gradually begin to succumb to smaller and slighter stimuli. The man whose boss has just threatened to fire him and whose house has developed a major structural fault will explode with violent anger when a button comes off his shirt. Eventually the unfortunate victim of ill fortune will be in a permanent state of alarm. He will be unable to differentiate between real problems and imaginary ones and his reactions to major and minor problems will become confused and probably irrational. He will be in a particularly bad way because he is uncertain and impotent. He would perhaps be in a healthier state if an earthquake had destroyed his home and his office. He would then have known the full extent of his problems and would, to a certain degree, have been able to help himself (and his neighbours) salvage remains from the wreckage. There would be something he could do.

The following table lists in order of precedence some of the problems commonly causing stress. (The table is partly based on information taken from 'The Social Readjustment Rating Scale' by Holmes & Rahe, published in *Journal of Psychosomatic Research*, 1967.)

1 Death of spouse
2 Divorce
3 Marital separation
4 Imprisonment
5 Death of close relative
6 Personal injury or illness
7 Marriage
8 Being sacked at work
9 Retirement
10 Change in health of family member
11 Pregnancy
12 Sex difficulties
13 Gain of new family member
14 Change in financial state
15 Death of close friend
16 Change of job, or major change in responsibilities at work
17 Taking out a mortgage or a major loan
18 Son or daughter leaving home
19 Trouble with in-laws
20 Outstanding personal achievement
21 Spouse begins or stops work
22 Starting or leaving school
23 Change in living conditions, working conditions, home or habits

24 Minor violation of the law – e.g. traffic violation
25 Taking out a small loan
26 Going on holiday, celebrating Christmas etc.


# ENVIRONMENTAL PRESSURES
## City life

Cities attract people as lamps attract moths and quite often prove just as fatal. Shelley wrote that, 'Hell is a city much like London, a populous and a smoky city' and evidence is accumulating fast to support the view that living in a city is dangerous in many ways. There are, to begin with, the simple physical disadvantages of living in a densely populated area. Inevitably the flow of traffic will be thick and slow. Road traffic accidents involving pedestrians are common in conditions like this and less spectacular damage, caused by pollutants from motor vehicles, can be equally fatal. There is evidence showing that the lead contained in vehicular exhausts can cause brain damage and that thousands of children living in cities may be classed as educationally subnormal because of damage caused by lead from petrol. As a result of the air pollution associated with large cities many chest diseases develop more often in city dwellers than in country folk. Bronchitis is a disease very common among city folk but relatively rare among villagers, even those who smoke. Similarly the incidence of lung cancer, often caused by pollutants, is four times as high in large cities as in rural areas.

Big city noise is also difficult to get away from. The noise of cars, buses and lorries, the noise of machinery and office equipment and the noise of several million radio and television sets provides a background against which can be set the more spectacular noises of aircraft and road menders.

If the ears of the city dweller suffer so do the eyes. The roads are plastered with instructions for both motorists and pedestrians and there are few walls or windows not decorated with advertisements clamouring for attention. There is no overall plan and although the bright lights undoubtedly have their attractions these visual insults add so much to the ugliness of the modern city that they often have a real effect on the general state of mind of the city dweller.

Even though city dwellers are usually economically better-off than their compatriots outside the city limits some suffer a lower standard of living. Travelling takes up much time and money and generally detracts from the quality of life rather than adding to it. Regular congestion, long queues, fatiguing journeys and overcrowded buses and trains all add to the burdens the city dweller must carry.

Vandalism is a common problem in most cities. According to a plastic surgeon in Manchester the major cause of facial injuries in the North West of England is no longer motoring accidents but fights and football violence. When six hundred children in Liverpool were interviewed it was found that nearly half of them had broken a street lamp in the previous six months. A survey in London showed that half of the people questioned did not feel that it was safe to go out alone in central London at night. In one month in 1975 Kent Council reported losses caused by vandals totalling £198,000. Repairing the damage done by vandals costs British Rail over £1 million per year and costs the GPO about £½ million per year. All this is just the tip of an iceberg. One survey showed that only three per cent of all incidents of vandalism find their way into the official crime statistics. The answer most vandals give when asked why they destroy is, 'for fun'. They do it because they are bored, a common problem in modern cities, and boredom is as genuine a cause of distress as fear or anxiety.

City dwellers do not share any sense of community spirit with their fellow citizens. There is, in a big city, no feeling of 'belonging'. In a fascinating piece of research published in 1969 Dr Zimbardo reported how he had left a motor car in a street in New York with the bonnet up. Within seven minutes pedestrians began to dismantle the car and sixty-four hours later there was nothing left but the bare hulk. When a similar vehicle was left in a similar type of neighbourhood in a smaller city the car was still in the same condition sixty-four hours later apart from the fact that a considerate passer-by had lowered the bonnet during a shower.

Many city areas are deteriorating rapidly. As the buildings become older and more dilapidated the wealthy and influential move out. As a result political pressure to maintain public service falls and so the downfall of the community continues. In due course muggers and hoodlums move in to take over the area. Aware of this process of decay, many who live in cities are almost permanently waiting for the initial sign of deterioration in their own community.

Because of the pressures of city life city dwellers fall ill more often and need more artificial support than people living in country areas. Each year the average citizen in Stockholm takes 23.3 days sick leave, whereas in the remainder of Sweden the average is 16.9 days per year. Alcoholism is much more common in cities than in suburban or rural areas.

The healthiest life is that of a citizen living in a small caring community where problems are shared and relationships are developed, established and respected. Nevertheless, there are many millions of people who live and thrive in cities. They survive happily because they enjoy the advantages (cultural, social and economic) of city life and because for them these advantages outweigh the disadvantages I have described. When assessing the factors causing stress in your life it is important to remember that many situations and activities which produce stress also produce pleasure and satisfaction.

## Commerce

Planned obsolescence both of ideas and of products puts pressure on consumers. In addition to useful labour-saving devices there are many gimmicks and gadgets marketed. Many gadgets are powered by electricity and consist of highly sophisticated pieces of machinery which can easily go wrong. Often muscle-powered tools would do the same job for a fraction of the cost if they were available. Succumbing to high pressure advertising, together with a desire to build up one's status with the neighbours and the shortage of simple goods, means that many families own motorised lawn mowers when a simple hand-pushed mower would be easier to handle, cheaper to buy and run, and far more reliable.

Many large companies are seemingly unconcerned about the pressures they put on customers to boost sales. One company making potato peelers painted the handle in such a way that it would be thrown away with the potato peelings. Many companies confuse shoppers by offering different sized packs at widely differing prices. It is difficult for the harassed shopper to decide to buy 8 fish fingers for 54 pence, 6 fish fingers for 45 pence, or 250 grams of fish fingers for 48 pence.

## Communications
Bad news spreads round the world far more quickly than it has ever done before. An earthquake, flood, kidnapping, assassination or major disaster will be news in every country of the world within a few hours. Many viewers, listeners and readers find all this bad news disturbing and find it difficult to understand just why good news is hardly news at all.

## Housing
High rise blues – the problems and depressions which gnaw at families leading an imprisoned existence in towering blocks of flats – have had ample publicity. There is solid evidence to support those who condemn these buildings as unsuitable. People who live in blocks of flats are not only in physical danger, they are likely to suffer mental and psychological strains unknown to people living in houses, bungalows and smaller blocks of flats.

The most obvious physical danger is the fire risk. There have been several gas explosions in large blocks of flats and in some cases rescue work has been hampered because a blast has wrecked a stairway. It is frightening to think of what could happen to people living on top floors beyond the reach of firemen's ladders. There is also the danger of structural faults. Many inhabitants of high rise flats worry about these dangers.

A doctor serving in the British army has made a very convincing study of the effect of living in a block of flats on the incidence of illness. He divided his patients into two groups, those living in flats and those living in terraced houses. He studied them carefully for ten weeks and found that there were 57 per cent more episodes of new illness among the people living in flats than among the people in houses. The incidence of respiratory infections was strikingly higher among flat-dwellers, and there was even a direct link with the height at which they lived. The higher the storey number, the more likely a woman or child was to develop a respiratory infection.

This researcher also showed a much higher incidence of psychoneurotic disturbance among people in flats than among house-dwellers. Psychoneurotic illnesses were most frequent among flat-dwelling women between twenty and thirty years old, nearly three times more than among women living in terraced houses. In the flats, there were 63 episodes of new illness among each thousand women living on the ground floor, and 127 among each thousand in third floor flats. The investigator noted in his report that he thought the essential difference between the flat-dwellers and the house-dwellers was that the people in the houses had much easier access to the world around and a greater opportunity to make friends.

Those in flats were more isolated, and people living in flats received notably less help from their neighbours than those in terraced houses. Thus it seems that people are still strongly rooted emotionally to the soil, and that living in tall blocks of flats is unhealthy in many different ways. Architects and politicians who were originally involved in the development of high rise flats now agree about this. In the UK local authorities have been instructed to halt the building of multistorey blocks of flats and concentrate on buildings with no more than three storeys.

## Noise

We are most of us more or less permanently surrounded by noise. It disturbs concentration and communications, produces fatigue and bad temper and results in damaged hearing. When exposed to noise we often become aggressive. When the level of noise is around or below fifty decibels it is very peaceful. Ordinary conversation produces about 60 decibels and a lorry and a washing machine will both produce eighty to ninety decibels. When the noise produced exceeds one hundred decibels (as it does in factories and at pop concerts) appreciable hearing loss

11

may be produced. Noise results in the tensing of muscles and that, in turn produces headaches and high blood pressure. Even the *absence* of noise may prove annoying. Noises which appear at unpredictable times can produce pressure when present or absent. During periods of quietness the unfortunate sufferer may be tensed, prepared for another bout of noise.

The disturbance caused by a noise depends upon the source as well as its predictability. The noise of her husband's car coming into the drive late at night when he has been away on a business trip will be welcomed by a faithful, worried wife. The noise he makes when slamming the car doors and opening and shutting the garage doors is not disturbing. On the other hand the same noises made by a neighbour's son returning home from a party can be extremely annoying.

Transport vehicles and factories are the two most important causes of noise. Because of the continuous high level of noise, however, these noise producers are likely to be relatively acceptable. The noise of an incoming aeroplane, which is unpredictable and individually identifiable, as well as of little relevance to most of the people it disturbs, may awaken considerable opposition.

Some noises may actually reduce pressure and strain. By the judicious use of audible wallpaper it is possible to exclude distracting unpredictable noises. Many students today use taped music or even radio music programmes to help them concentrate. The steady noise level is less disturbing than the miscellaneous noises which are often more or less impossible to exclude (the noise of the telephone, the distant television, traffic, construction industries and even children playing).

It is often possible to protect oneself against outside noise by using double glazing and sound proofing. Even the judicious building of book shelves can prove a useful sound barrier. Muffles on vehicles, screens and embankments separating traffic from houses and many other techniques can help reduce the interaction between noise and people. Those citizens who are annoyed by loud unpredictable noises usually find that even if it isn't possible to control or reduce the noise, the strain it produces can be alleviated a little by protesting. One of the stress-inducing features of external noise is that there is usually nothing most of us can do about it. Protesting helps to reduce the inevitable feeling of frustration.

## Overcrowding

Although one must always study animal experiments with suspicion and scepticism before applying the results to human beings, it is interesting to note that putting chickens into overcrowded quarters causes coronary arteriosclerosis, overcrowded mice develop high blood pressure and when animals which normally live wild are kept in zoos they develop heart disease. In one famous experiment 134 baboons were placed in an enclosure which measured 100 feet by 60 feet. After 6 years 33 of the 35 females had died and 62 of the 99 males had died. No less than 30 of the female baboons had died from injuries. Only 15 young baboons were born and of these only 1 survived to the age of six months. Another researcher who worked with rats showed that overcrowding caused a breakdown of social mores and that the dominant rats developed criminal tendencies.

Studies done on human beings have shown that crime rates, the incidence of vascular disease and mental disease (and levels of infective disease of course) all rise when overcrowding gets worse. People who live in overcrowded circumstances lose their sense of personal identity, develop a tendency to accept things passively without protest and paradoxically often suffer from loneliness. In overcrowded circumstances differences which might otherwise be tolerated become unbearable.

Despite all this evidence there are, of course, many who find crowded areas stimulating, and quiet areas boring. One man's stressor is another man's pleasure.

## Population structure

It took many thousands of years for the world's population to reach its first billion. The second billion was reached after another hundred years and the third was added in a mere thirty years. It is expected that the world's population will have reached seven billion by the year 2000. The growth of the world's population in recent years can be vividly illustrated by the fact that in 1750 there were 800 million people living on the earth, by 1900 there were 1,600 million and by 1964 the world's population had reached 3,200 million. This population explosion has inevitably produced many problems and influenced the way we live and the pressures under which we survive.

Changes in the age structure of the population have, for example, been quite dramatic. In 1931 less than 10 per cent of the population were over retirement age in Britain. By 1974 the figure had reached 17 per cent. In other words, allowing for an increase in the size of the overall population, the number of retired persons had doubled. In 1931 there were 51 people under the age of 15 or over retirement age for every 100 people of working age. By 1974 there were 68 people under 15 and over the retirement age for every 100 people of working age. It is clear that the pressures on working men and women today are much greater in that they must care for an increasing section of the population.

Despite these changes in population structure facilities for looking after the weak and financially helpless elderly have changed very little. Parents of young families often find that as their own offspring grow up and leave home they themselves are left with the responsibility of caring for their own parents. The middle years that they might have expected to be peaceful and restful will be neither and they will have no chance of preparing for their own years of retirement.

Another result of the change in the structure of the population has been the shrinking of the average family size. Economic, cultural and medical factors have all led to the reduction in the number of children in the average family. In Britain, for example, the average family contained seven children in 1860. A hundred years later the average family contained but two children. Smaller families mean less sibling support for children and parents and sometimes leads to overprotectiveness by parents.

**Television**
The television set in the corner of almost every living room in the land plays an extraordinarily important role in the lives of

almost all of us. Even those viewers over the age of thirty who grew up in the now almost unimaginable pre-television era treat the silver screen as a member of the family. Viewers under thirty, who have grown up with the television set as an almost constant companion treat the screen with a frightening mixture of awe and affection. The television set is an education aid at school, an entertainment at home and a reliable companion come rain or shine.

A report in the *Journal of the American Medical Association* recently showed that by the time they reach the age of eighteen American children will have been sitting in front of the television set for something like 15,000 hours – whereas they will have spent 11,000 hours sitting in the classroom at school. There are no comparable British figures but if children start watching television at the age of three they only have to watch 3 hours a day to reach a total of 15,000 hours by their late teens. My observations suggest that the average British child does spend 3 hours a day in front of the television set.

The same journal also suggested that by the age of eighteen American children have been exposed to no fewer than 350,000 television commercials. In Britain there are two advertisement-free channels and commercial stations show fewer advertisements but it nevertheless seems likely that British children will have viewed something like 100,000 advertisements before they are old enough to vote. In addition to these commercials exhortations there will have been messages from commentators and politicians.

The Nielson Index figures suggest that the American school-leaving child will have witnessed no fewer than 18,000 murders on the television set in his home and will have been able to view countless detailed robberies, bombings, torturings and beatings. Some of these evil deeds will have been fictional, some will have been factual. A total of 146 articles published in US scientific journals, dealing in all with approximately 10,000 children and young people from every conceivable background, have all suggested that violence on television turns young people into more aggressive citizens. American doctors, psychologists and students of human behaviour now seem convinced that television programmes, and many of the advertisements, are harmful. Researchers have shown convincingly that children learn aggressive behaviour from watching aggressive actions on the television screen and that evidence on television tends to reduce a child's normal inhibition against aggressive behaviour.

According to *Time* magazine (10 October, 1977) an American defence attorney has argued that a client of his charged with murder 'was suffering from and acted under the influence of prolonged, intense, involuntary, subliminal television intoxication.' The lawyer, Ellis Rubin, claimed that 'the tube became his client's parent, school and church.' In another murder case the accused testified that he and his partner killed four people after watching a television dramatisation of the Manson murders.

There seems little doubt that the television set does influence the way we live and the attitudes we favour. The TV set is a powerful tool in the hands of all those anxious to manipulate and even when used by those with no ulterior motive at all it can have a powerful effect on our lives. There should perhaps be an Act passed instructing the manufacturers of television sets to fix a notice to each set with the message 'Warning: this set may damage your mind.' Or perhaps it might be wise to fit television sets with devices which meant that after each programme the television set switched itself off and needed to be turned back on again. That way perhaps there might be some control over indiscriminate viewing of dull and unedifying programmes which simply encourage indolence, boredom and all the associated stress diseases.

Having said so much about the disadvantages of television it is only fair to add that discriminating viewing provides many millions with education and entertainment and that the lonely, the disabled and the elderly often regard the television set as a welcome friend who relieves their loneliness and boredom.

### Transport
Improved methods of modern transport make it quicker and perhaps simpler to travel but no less onerous. Motor car journeys are tiring, boring and dangerous for drivers and passen-

gers. Adults and children are kept cooped up in their metal box for hours at a time; conversation is often impossible because of the need of the driver to concentrate and the noise of the engine and the tyres on the road. Driving motor vehicles in heavy traffic is extremely exhausting both physically and mentally. A study of London bus staff showed that the drivers were much more likely than the conductors to suffer from illnesses such as cardiac disease. Travel by aeroplane is also likely to cause disease. For both crew and passengers, taking off and landing are the most worrying times. Large numbers of international travellers need tranquillisers to make those most dangerous moments acceptable.

It isn't only the physical risks associated with travel which produce strain, however. Today's forms of transport are speedy and travellers can cross whole continents in a few hours. In the hustle and bustle of the twentieth-century business world where tomorrow is never as good as today the traveller may be expected to begin work within minutes of his arrival in a different climate, on a different time scale and with his personal body clock completely confused.

It is quite possible that the diarrhoea or constipation suffered by many travellers are not caused by a change in the water or food consumed but by the travelling itself and by the change in surroundings. Both travel and new surroundings can produce the symptoms of physiological stress and result in physical changes.

## SOURCES OF SOCIAL STRAINS
### Bureaucracy
Those in our society who have responsibility rarely seem to have authority and those with authority seem to lack personal responsibility. I personally believe that authority without responsibility and responsibility without authority have led to much of the anger and frustration against the system within which we must all live.

Doctors working in hospitals who have considerable personal responsibility, are very short on authority. They have responsibility for the safety of their patients but they do not have the authority to ensure that the equipment and facilities they need are made available. Hospital administrators, on the other hand, have a great deal of authority but no personal responsibility for their actions. The same is true of almost all nationalized industries and of the civil service. There is an unrealistic separation of responsibility from authority.

The collective power of our bureaucrats is extremely frustrating and debilitating for all of us (including the bureaucrats themselves when their personal responsibilities are affected). On an international, national and municipal level bureaucracies are demanding and unbending. Major industries, the police force and the hospital service all exhibit signs of having divorced authority from responsibility.

## Discrimination

Race, sex, religion and age are but four of the qualities likely to lead to discrimination. Unfortunate possession of the wrong qualifications in any of these categories can lead to discrimination by employers, landlords, banks and even governments. Even though liberal attitudes have spread in most developed countries there is still an extraordinary amount of discrimination practised. For example, many men and women are forced to retire when they reach the age of sixty-five, sixty, or even fifty-five although they may want to carry on working and be physically and mentally capable of doing so.

## Emancipation

The emancipation of women has put a strain on members of both sexes. Women are now expected to be less emotional and more businesslike, to achieve success as individuals rather than as members of a marriage partnership. This means finding status at work while holding on to status at home. Managing two lives, with their separate demands, can prove a great burden to many women.

Men may find that the strength of their position at home has been eroded. The nineteenth-century husband and father expected to be admired by his wife and respected by his children. Even at the beginning of this century most most expected a relation-

18

ship of this sort. Today's adult male may have to put up with a critical wife who has a more successful career than he has and with rebellious, free-thinking children who have little or no respect for him, his work and his ideals. Today it is only the traditional adult Arab male who can expect to find an obedient wife who speaks only when invited so to do.

The disappearance of long established values and the distorting of traditional relationships between men and women put both the male and the female of the species under pressure. Nevertheless, there are undoubtedly many women who feel that the liberation movement has freed them from the stresses caused by discrimination.

## Work

Blue collar workers, executives and professionals are all subjected to pressures. Shift work, redundancy, take-overs, the pyramidal power structure, responsibility without authority, early retirement, excessive bureaucracy and boredom all create their own problems.

Naturally the pressures which affect workers in different jobs vary a great deal. The self-employed craftsman doesn't have to worry about going to work when he wants to watch a football game but because he hasn't got an employer to look after him he will probably carry on working when he feels sick. The self-employed man, be he businessman or professional man, will very probably work longer hours than his employed neighbour. Many entrepreneurs are quite unable to relax and feel frustrated when they can't manage a twelve hour day for seven days a week.

Boredom is a serious problem for workers in many factories. It has been shown that when small animals called planaria are given simple, repetitive tasks to do to find water they commit suicide rather than carry on. Some factories have tried to eliminate repetitive tasks by building exra machinery and by giving workers the chance to participate more directly in the preparation of an identifiable product. Saab and Volvo, the Swedish car manufacturers, both give their workers a chance to make their work more pleasing by allowing them to build cars in small groups rather than in long lines working on conveyor belts. An American telephone company which had thirty girls working on the production of telephone directories gave each girl the job of producing a single directory rather than making the girls work as a team on each book. They found that their employees got a great deal more satisfaction from their work.

Other factories have found that giving workers variety, responsibility and the opportunity to control the quality of their own work improves worker satisfaction, output and quality. Allowing workers to decide when they will work and how fast they will work can help. On the other hand when work is exceedingly boring and frustrating (as in the British car industry) workers become unwilling to do what they are supposed to do and become simply greedy for more money. Little is expected of them at work and so they give little.

There is commercial wisdom in keeping workers satisfied since many strikes develop simply because employees find that only industrial action offers them excitement, glamour, and any feeling of control over their own environment. Blue collar workers with simple jobs are sometimes so frustrated by their work that in addition to failing to turn up they actually commit sabotage. Unions which worry about pay, conditions and fringe benefits should perhaps worry more about variety, dignity, skill, respect, status, responsibility and adding a 'meaning' to the work their members do. Too often workers have no idea what they are producing. They may go off to the shops and then complain that the very item they've helped produce is shoddy and unreliable. Working hours in the United States have fallen from an average of fifty-eight a week in 1894 to thirty-eight a week today and yet workers are looking for even shorter working hours with longer breaks and opportunities to take time off from work.

Many jobs in service industries produce pressure. Traffic wardens, for example, whose work is unpopular, suffer a great deal. One woman I treated was a nervous wreck after papering cars with tickets for a few months. She gave in her notice and refused to apply any more tickets while she worked out her last few weeks. Telephone operators at busy exchanges, and supermarket check-out girls are often under heavy pressure which can prove damaging.

Work should provide self-esteem, satisfaction, and financial security, and should be intellectually and physically satisfying. It should not be inordinately dangerous, there should be a visible and identifiable end product and it should produce satis fying inter-personal relationships. Ideally the worker should be allowed responsibility for arranging his own employment and given as much independence as possible.

Unfortunately, however, few employers seem concerned to provide employment of such a nature. The pyramidal power structure is common in large factories. Political and industrial power is centralized and all major decisions are made at a head office which may be thousands of miles away from the action. The pyramidal power structure encourages the proliferation of 'yes men' and 'gofers' and the exclusion of workers with initiative and creative intelligence.

Movement up or down the ladder produces special problems of its own. An employee climbing the ladder may be resented by his colleagues unless he achieves enough status to be used as a friend in power or so much national fame that his friendship becomes a point of pride. Promotion to the position of foreman may take a man into an extremely difficult area. His former colleagues now regard him as one of 'them' and his management colleagues may still regard him as a member of the general work force. As is so well described in 'The Peter Principle' by Dr Laurence J. Peter and Raymond Hull, men and women are often over-promoted; being given work that they are incapable of doing. The principle is that 'In a hierarchy every employee tends to rise to his level of incompetence.' It is a brave employee who, when offered promotion that he cannot cope with, will refuse it.

Many large employers move their executives about with no regard for their well-being. Today's executives are yesterday's gypsies. To ensure loyalty and to keep their workers in the fold many large companies offer pension schemes, sickness insurance, free or cheap mortgages, free cars, school fees and so on. The employee with all these fringe benefits finds it more difficult to leave his employer or to risk offending the establishment.

Large companies don't like independent employees who moonlight or have incomes of their own.

Large employers, be they independent or nationalized, tend to develop bureaucracies of their own. Those who are trying to do real work within the bureaucratic framework may find life extremely frustrating. After the British National Health Service was reorganized the amount of paperwork involved in implementing a minor repair job grew to a bizarre extent. I saw as patients a number of engineers and nurses who found the excessive bureaucracy so frustrating that it caused many symptoms of stress disease. Many people seem prepared to ignore common sense and obey the letter of the local law. Formophilia is seemingly contagious.

The job you do influences dramatically the chances you take of dying from certain disorders. In the table below the four columns show deaths from (A) coronary disease, (B) duodenal ulcer, (C) suicide, (D) stroke. A standardized mortality ratio of 100 would be an average for all workers. (These figures are taken from the British Registrar General's Occupational Mortality tables.)

|  | A | B | C | D |
|---|---|---|---|---|
| Farmers, foresters, fishermen | 69 | 71 | 117 | 84 |
| Miners, quarrymen | 98 | 116 | 107 | 105 |
| Labourers | 118 | 176 | 188 | 138 |
| Clerical workers | 119 | 99 | 94 | 107 |
| Administrators and Managers | 95 | 50 | 63 | 73 |
| Professional artists | 96 | 58 | 94 | 85 |
| Gardeners and groundsmen | 82 | 90 | 81 | 119 |
| Ships' Officers | 152 | 110 | 125 | 111 |
| Civil Servants | 118 | 107 | 125 | 446 |
| MPs, Senior Government Officers | 97 | 86 | 44 | 30 |
| Company directors | 758 | 485 | 700 | 1925 |
| Doctors | 118 | 110 | 67 | 176 |
| Accountants | 93 | 92 | 31 | 91 |
| Clergymen | 90 | 83 | 60 | 53 |
| Judges, Lawyers | 93 | 84 | 100 | 133 |

## Fashion

There are many social strains caused by variations in fashions which are totally unrelated to women's clothes. For example, it has been unfashionable for women to breast feed their children for some years now. One common reason for this move away from nature is that women fear that the shape of their breasts will be less appealing if they are used as functional rather than decorative items. As a consequence of this unnatural fashion mothers and babies are both deprived of inestimably valuable comfort.

Physical punishment of misbehaved children by parents and teachers is another activity which drifts in and out of fashion. When it is not fashionable for parents to spank or even chastise their erring offspring everyone suffers. The parents suffer because they feel frustrated and thwarted. They know that they ought to punish and they feel that a good hiding might clear the air; but they are worried about the long-term effects such a punishment might have. They worry lest their child may grow up to hate them. The result is that the child either has to put up with bad-tempered, sulky parents (a much longer lasting and more damaging punishment) or suffers because he has no opportunity to learn the boundaries within which he must live his life. The child who is not spanked may have to put up with a long lasting deprivation of love and affection. It is less stressful for a child to receive a short, sharp punishment which ends the matter completely than for child and parent to endure a long drawn out battle.

## The housewives' syndrome

The modern housewife is under many pressures that her predecessors would have never imagined. Surrounded by laboursaving gadgets and aids which give her more free time but less satisfaction from homekeeping chores the housewife is a common sufferer from stress. She becomes bored, because she has little to do except operate her machines and follow the instructions on packets of cake mix, and frustrated because of the apparent insignificance of her role. Housewives in their twenties, thirties and forties are the commonest consumers of tranquillizers.

The modern young family often lives on an estate where the housewife has few friends or relatives to turn to and the contemporary architects' attempts to provide citizens with privacy at all costs has meant that many homes are effectively prisons. The breakdown of the larger family unit and the tendency for ambitious young couples to move away from the areas in which they have their roots has added to the problem. In addition, children quickly learn independence and through the mass media follow values and ideals put forward by their peers rather than their parents.

Is it any wonder that young housewives often exhibit signs and symptoms of stress?

## Marriage

Although marriage undoubtedly reduces strain for a great many people who value the opportunity to share their good and bad fortune, it is all too easy to produce evidence showing that for many people marriage is a source of tremendous strain. One cause of strain is the undoubted fact that men and women often have different priorities. The malfunctioning washing machine is just as important to a housewife as a multi-million dollar deal to her husband. Failure to understand one another's problems is a common cause of marital distress.

Divorce is relatively simple today and although the dissolution of an unhappy marriage is undoubtedly a relief for many partners we must remember that many of those whose marriages have been dissolved live alone and virtually friendless. These people suffer a great deal and research has shown that divorced men and women share with widows and widowers a high incidence of 'stress' diseases.

## Religion

Religion may relieve strain by offering emotional and spiritual support to those in need but it also produces strains of its own. Changes in religious customs and contradictions between religious and social mores, for example, may have a tremendously destructive effect on those dependent upon religious support for moral and spiritual strength. Members of the Roman Catholic Church have suffered great torment during the recent long discussions about the rights and wrongs of contraception. On a more parochial basis, the change from Latin Mass to a more modern version has also put many establishment figures within the church under pressure.

## Sex

In 1860 most girls began to menstruate and to develop secondary sexual characteristics (breasts, plump buttocks, pubic hair, and so on) at the age of sixteen to seventeen years. By 1960 the majority of girls were maturing between the age of twelve and thirteen years. With each decade that passes girls mature about four months earlier. It seems that by 1980 most girls will begin to menstruate and develop breast tissue before the age of twelve years. Although for obvious reasons it is more difficult to decide just when boys become young men there is no reason to assume that the changes which have taken place in the female part of the population have not also taken place in the male half.

At the same time as their physical development has come at an earlier and earlier age young people of both sex have come under increasing pressure to marry later and to postpone natural desires and urges. Despite the freedom of the 'permissive society' and the availability of the contraceptive pill, parental attitudes still produce powerful and destructive feelings of guilt in many young people physically well capable of enjoying a perfectly satisfactory sex life but legally and morally forbidden to do so.

Sex offers an additional strain to the modern man and woman. The sex marketeers are working hard to convince each one of us that everyone *else* is devoted to sex. It is far more acceptable to admit publicly that you enjoy wrapping your neighbour's wife up in black plastic than to admit that you spend Saturday evenings curled up with a good book while your own wife, fully clothed, does her knitting. Citizens who enjoy sex but find that it fits into their lives alongside other pleasures rather than colouring their every thought may feel cheated, thwarted or even incompetent.

## PERSONAL PAINS
### Age
An individual's age may have an extraordinarily powerful in-

fluence upon the pressures under which that individual must exist.

Children have easy access to information of all kinds through television, radio, magazines and newspapers and as a result a child and his family are under powerful outside influences while the links between the child's immediate family and other members of the family have weakened.

Families are smaller than they used to be, mothers commonly go to work and fathers often work shifts. Inevitably, therefore, outside support is needed. Youth Groups and Clubs satisfy the children who enjoy organized activities. Many find companionship and support from gangs. Inevitably there is conflict between the demands of parents and peers. Babies and infants are weaned earlier, separated from their parents at an early age by being sent to play groups and specially organized schools. In relatively few families do parents and children ever play games together. The television set has more or less put an end to musical evenings. At the same time, as a result of political manoeuvres schoolchildren are subjected to inflexible curricula and a lack of stimulating competition in the classroom. Paradoxically they may have an excess of competition on the sports field.

As they reach their teens children are under tremendous pressure. Teenagers have to cope with an increase in educational pressures, the prospect of employment and unemployment, the mysteries of sex, marriage and even parenthood. They are expected to be responsible but given little or no responsibility for their own lives. Children whose physical or mental attributes lie outside the normal range are under special pressures. On top of all this there are the changes in hormone levels. Children whose parents move from area to area as their careers grow have to suffer changes of school, teacher and friends. Children of immigrants must frequently act as linguistic and cultural interpreters. In their late teens youngsters must cope with the academic and social pressures of college life. Many find these burdens intolerable and the number who find death a preferable alternative seems to grow each year.

Young business executives, young professional men and

26

indeed young people in all walks of life have a hard job acquiring any position with power and responsibility. Experience and contacts are more valuable in many circles than initiative, expertise and ambition. The result is that except for the entrepreneurs young men and women in their twenties and thirties suffer tremendous frustrations. It is a surprise to realize that Napoleon was an officer in the French army at the age of fifteen, a Brigadier at twenty-four and at twenty-six in command of the French army in Italy, opposing the Sardinians and the Austrians. We should remember that Hannibal led his army across the Alps at the age of twenty-nine, Joan of Arc led the French army to victory at Orleans in 1429 at the age of 17, Florence Nightingale was in charge of the hospital at Scutari at the age of thirty-four, William Pitt the Younger was Prime Minister at the age of twenty-four and that when he was thirty-three Thomas Jefferson (who lived to be eighty-three) wrote the American Declaration of Independence. At the outbreak of the first world war T. E. Lawrence was twenty-six years old. Dickens was twenty-four when he wrote *Pickwick Papers*.

The pressures are still there at the other end of the age spectrum. The elderly must often cope with enforced retirement, lack of status, failing health and financial insecurity.

Those in their middle years have the problem of coping with relatives at the two extremes of life.

## Personality
The personality of an individual greatly influences his response to any stressor. In the same situation one person may freeze, another cry and a third person remain calm and in control. Compulsive, aggressive people without confidence suffer badly when under pressure. Those who are able to show their emotions freely suffer less lasting damage.

An individual's personality is not simply dependent upon genetic factors. The environment within which an individual has existed while young must have a powerful effect if only because conditioning from experienced situations must affect behaviour and because a conscience is in reality nothing more or less than a personal view of expected social behaviour.

Hippocrates divided individuals into four main groups: the choleric, the phlegmatic, the sanguine and the melancholic. The choleric individual, classically physically weak and irritable is likely to be aggressive and susceptible to stomach upsets. The melancholic is more introspective, more emotional and more likely to worry. Both the melancholic and the choleric will suffer more obviously under pressure than the sanguine and the phlegmatic. The sanguine man is an extrovert who works and plays hard and is likely to suffer diseases caused by his way of life rather than by the pressures to which he is exposed. The phlegmatic individual is classically plump and rather slow seemingly calm but susceptible to heart disease.

Hans Eysenck describes the melancholic as an unstable introvert, the choleric as an unstable extrovert, the phlegmatic as a stable introvert and the sanguine as a stable extrovert. He allows, of course, that personality is only one of the factors which makes a man – the others including ability, luck and environment – but argues that sportsmen are often sanguine, criminals choleric, neurotics melancholic and scientists and businessmen phlegmatic.

## Illness

Any illness, physical or mental, real or imagined, lengthy or short-lived, life-threatening or mild, produces strain. In addition to the pain and weakness, sense of frustration and economic worry which accompany many illnesses there is the fear of death to be dealt with and the often unrequited need for support and encouragement from relatives, friends and nursing staff.

In general, acute physical illnesses attract more sympathy from those around than do chronic physical illnesses or mental illnesses. Disfiguring and grossly disabling diseases often frighten away would be sympathisers. Simple fractures and easily identifiable and curable disorders attract most support.

Another cause of strain is the fact that our communal medical knowledge often exceeds our practical capabilities. It is often most disturbing for patients and relatives to discover that a theoretically possible cure is practically unavailable. It is, for example, difficult to explain or understand why an artificial kidney may be made available for one patient but not for another.

## Desire for status

Every day we are all subjected to hundreds of messages from people wanting to tell us things. Twenty years ago the American investigator Vance Packard estimated that in an average day an ordinary American would receive 1,518 advertising messages. There are direct mail promotions and newspaper advertisements at breakfast, posters, hoardings and shop window displays on the way to work or to the shops, free journals and unsolicited telephone calls in the office; door to door salesmen call at home and television, radio and cinema programmes are all accompanied by advertisements which are variously insulting, boring, informative, intimidating, useful, condescending and revolting. Together the various advertisements add to the variety of outside stimuli clamouring for attention.

In recent years advertisements have even begun to appear from banks and other financial institutions offering to lend their customers money to spend on items both luxurious and frivolous. The banks encourage a feeling of desire on the part of the customer who is shown photographs of items he might not otherwise be able to afford and encouraged to borrow the necessary money even though he may not really be able to afford the necessary repayments.

No advertising programmes would work, of course, if the people seeing the advertisements were not receptive and if the advertisements themselves were not designed to appeal to the innate desires and expectations of the public. Some advertising programmes are designed to appeal to a man's sense of insecurity (for example, it is suggested that he won't smell right if he doesn't use the right soap, that he won't be acceptable in public unless he wears the right clothes) but the majority of advertisements appeal to our desire to accumulate and to own material goods as an outward sign of our success as human beings.

People buy bigger houses, faster cars, more complex radio

equipment, more expensive kitchen gadgets, more sophisticated gardening tools and more clothes than they really need because they are afraid that if they don't buy all these things they will lose status in the eyes of their friends and colleagues. Fashion houses which produce new designs do so in the certain knowledge that women will follow new designs, however outrageous, rather than appear in public dressed out of fashion. Different groups of society follow different fashions but the teenage girl wearing jeans and safety pins is following fashion just as devotedly as her middle-aged mother worrying about the height of her skirt and the depth of her cleavage. Those who create and advertise these new fashions heighten the awareness and material ambitions of their customers; they are not directly putting pressure on consumers to buy but they are encouraging consumers to put pressure on themselves.

It is not, of course, only material belongings which appeal to the status conscious. There are many more facets to status than wealth. Academic success enables many to achieve status and authority although of course we must not forget that the status which accompanies academic success is often present because the academic success promises a certain amount of accompanying material success!

Young people are encouraged by relatives to stay at school as long as possible and to obtain as many certificates as they can although they may be uninterested in the subjects they are studying and despite the fact that there are often no opportunities for them to use their hard-earned qualifications and that consequently they will be frustrated. Both parents and teachers encourage the children in their care to seek success. The children do so either because they find the prospect of success satisfying or because they wish to win approval and praise from parents and teachers. The academically weak are put under pressure to do well at sports. For example, junior and secondary school pupils, some only twelve or thirteen years old, are often encouraged to compete in international swimming competitions such as the Olympic Games. Young footballers and athletes are encouraged to enter competitions and to develop a competitive nature as early as possible. Even seven and eight year old footballers are made to play for their places in school and club sides and will be taught to analyse their performance after the match has finished. Young tennis players and golfers are encouraged to stand and practise for hours at a time in an attempt to achieve success, win prizes and gain the opportunity to earn money at the sport.

This aggressive attitude is not only likely to produce physical damage – it is also highly likely to produce psychological problems. The young swimmer who is an international celebrity at fourteen will be under great pressure to remain 'at the top'. As she fades with age she may find it extremely difficult to come to terms with her relative failures. The athletes who do not reach the top will be aware that they have failed their parents and disappointed their coaches and teachers.

The common factor which links the acquisition of material goods, academic certificates or sporting prizes is a desire for status; a desire to win respect and admiration. The academic seeking certificated success and the sportsman hoping to win prizes are both looking for success, for parental approval and for self-satisfaction. These are all laudable and very human aspirations without which life would be extremely dull but inevitably there are many who are prepared to take advantage of this demand and desire for recognition to make money. In marketing and advertising commercial products they are simply taking advantage of the pressures people put on themselves.

# Part Two
## The Counterstress Philosophy

Here we meet the ways in which the reader can recognize the symptoms of stress, we discuss the need for him to understand his own motives and priorities, and describe the many ways in which he can prepare himself, both physically and mentally, to counter stress.

# INTRODUCTION

If your motor car is in good condition it will take you many miles without trouble if you drive carefully and with restraint. If you drive too quickly, hurling the car around bad bends and over rough roads, or if you drive for long periods of time in heavy, slow moving traffic than the car will very probably break down. The human body behaves just like a motor car. Use it carefully and wisely and it will last without attention for long periods of time. If, however, the body is mis-used or subjected to unusual strains and pressures it is likely to show signs of wear and tear. The strains and pressures may be environmental, psychological or social.

Usually when these pressures begin to build up to dangerous levels the body's early warning signs of distress come into operation. A chest pain (see p. 126), headache (see p. 160), persistent diarrhoea (see p. 157) or skin rash (see p. 149) can all be early warning signs of trouble brewing. If these warning signs are ignored more drastic trouble may develop. If you ignore the temperature gauge on your car the engine may blow up and if anginal pains (see p. 126) are ignored a heart attack (see p. 161) may follow.

The man who has a heart attack can, presuming that he survives, take a hard close look at his life and decide what changes need to be made. If he makes the right changes then he will very probably make a good recovery but naturally it is much better to take action *before* a major crisis occurs. That is why the early warning signs of impending illness are so important. In the following section of this book I describe the various symptoms and signs which may herald the beginnings of a 'stress' disease. It is too simplistic to suggest that readers should simply ignore strains or learn to 'thrive on stress'. The truth is that to survive healthily in our society most of us need to develop an understanding of the factors causing stress, of the ways those factors can be controlled and of the ways in which we can prepare ourselves to cope with them successfully and effectively. The preparation of this aggressive defence is the basis of the counterstress philosophy.

# THE EARLY WARNING SIGNS

First, of course, it is necessary to know when problems are developing. You must learn to recognize when trouble is looming ahead. There are both physical and mental signs to be on the look out for. Most of us have a weak point and it is here that the first symptoms usually appear. For example, some people suffer from indigestion when worried or anxious while others develop headaches.

The most important physical early warning signs are:
> Chest pains (see p. 126)
> Diarrhoea persisting for more than a few days (see p. 157)
> Headaches (see p. 160)
> Indigestion (see p. 171)
> Insomnia (see p. 172)
> Palpitations (see p. 180)
> Tiredness (often a result of insomnia)

The mental signs which most frequently occur when pressure is too great are:
> Inability to relax properly at any time
> Intolerance of noise or other disturbing stimuli
> Irritability and short temper
> A poor memory
> Inability to concentrate
> Reduction in will power
> Uncontrollable emotions, particularly frequent crying
> Inability to finish tasks which have been started
> Impulsive behaviour
> Over-reacting to little things

In the third part of this book I have listed the commonest diseases caused by stress. People suffering from one or more of these disorders should consider it likely that stress has been an important factor in the development of their disease. Reducing your exposure to stress or increasing your ability to resist the harmful physical and mental effects of pressures will prove a valuable adjunct to medically prescribed treatment methods. Without either reducing the level of stress to which you are exposed or increasing your own ability to withstand distressing pressures it is extremely likely that once treated and cured your problems will reappear. Simply treating signs and symptoms of illness is like repairing the damaged bodywork of a motor car but not bothering to do anything about the faulty brakes which had originally caused the accident.

## IDENTIFY THE FACTORS WHICH CAUSE STRESS

Before the problems causing distress can be solved they must be identified. Only when they have been identified can action be taken to minimize their effect or can specific forms of treatment be initiated. The first part of this book describes in some detail the various categories of problems likely to produce signs of distress.

Until the causative factors have been properly identified all that can be done is to treat signs of distress symptomatically. Chewing antacid tablets to help cure indigestion or swallowing pain killers to treat a headache only provide a short-term cure. If your car has a leaky radiator hose you can solve the problem in the short term by merely pouring more water into the radiator. This will not, however, provide any lasting solution to the problem.

To identify the factors causing your stress study the first part of this book carefully, writing down problems which you think apply to you. Understanding and identifying the problems in your life enables you to be prepared for them and to deal with them.

Making a list of your own personal sources of stress will help. Take a look at the list on page six in Part One of this book and decide which events have affected your life in the last year. What problems are you facing at home? What difficulties are there at work? What about hobbies and leisure time activities? Do you feel rested and refreshed after spending time on your hobby or do you just feel worse than ever? What about personal relationships? Do you have problems with the people you work with? Are your problems financial? How much does your immediate environment affect you?

## YOUR COUNTERSTRESS CHECKLIST

Check your exposure to stressful situations and stimuli with the following questionnaire. Every 'yes' indicates a point of exposure and potential weakness.

### Your physical environment

Do you live in a city?

Do you have to commute to work?

Is the office or factory or shop where you work usually noisy?

Do you have to avoid going out alone at night where you live?

Do your neighbours keep to themselves and avoid offering help to others if possible?

Do you own equipment recently bought that you don't really need?

When you mow the lawn does it take longer to prepare the mower than to actually cut the grass?

Do you live in a block of flats?

Can you hear your neighbour's TV set and squabbles at night?

Do you live near to a busy road?

Do you live near to an airport?

Do you live near to a large factory?

Do you ever have to raise your voice to make yourself heard in your home because of noises outside?

Do you have to share an entrance with other people?

Do you wish you had a room of your own to which you could retire when you are looking for a little peace and quiet?

Do you end up watching television most evenings because you don't have anything else to do?

Is the TV set switched on by others when you would rather be doing something else?

Do you have to travel long distances when you would rather stay at home?

Do you spend more than half an hour a day travelling?

Do you fly though you hate flying?

Are you always in a hurry when on business trips?

**Your social environment**

Do you wish you had more responsibility?

Do you wish you had less responsibility?

Do you get frustrated at work?

Are your activities restricted because of your age?

Did you have to retire earlier than you wanted to?

Do you wish you could have retired earlier?

Do you think your sex has affected your promotion chances at work?

Do you think your sex has affected your ability to raise a mortgage?

Do you believe your religion has adversely affected your career?

Do you think your race or skin colour has adversely affected your career?

Do you regularly suffer social discrimination?

Do you wish your spouse understood you better?

Do you feel that you are competing with your spouse?

Do you feel that your spouse should respect you more?

Do you feel that your children should respect you more?

Do you worry about what might happen if you fall sick?

Do you find it difficult to relax and forget about work at night?

Do you find it difficult to relax and forget about work at weekends?

Do you regularly get bored at work?

Do you find yourself fighting bureaucrats every day?

Do you have a rushed lunch as a regular thing?

Do you regularly get home late from work?

Do you take work home with you?

Do you have to cancel holidays because of your work?

Do you find yourself having to be nice to people you cannot stand?

Do you find your work unsatisfying?

Do you believe your firm produces shoddy goods or provides people with an unsatisfactory service?

Do you often wonder whether it's all worthwhile?

Do you wonder exactly what it is your firm makes?

Do you go to work purely and simply to earn a living?

When work becomes interesting do you have to hand over to someone else?

Do you find it impossible to talk to your boss?

Do you believe your boss is incompetent?

Do you worry about what will happen when you retire?

Do you believe you would have difficulty in obtaining similar employment elsewhere?

Does your firm own your house?

Is your mortgage linked to your job?

Do you earn less than your neighbours?

Do you spend every penny you earn?

Do you usually have an overdraft?

Do you worry a lot about what other people think?

Do you listen carefully to all advice given on TV and radio and in newspapers and magazines?

How often do you leave the house without saying goodbye to your spouse?

Does your spouse seem too busy to discuss your day in the evenings?

Do you sometimes feel marriage was a mistake?

Do you feel that you fail to uphold the principles of your religion?

Do you feel that your sex drive is considerably higher than the normal?

Do you feel that your sex drive is rather lower than normal?

Do you find sex with your regular partner unsatisfying?

Do you envy other people's sex lives?

Do you feel guilty about your sexual preferences?

## You

Do you feel that life has passed you by?

Do you have no real friends with whom you can discuss personal problems?

Do you feel that you could have done something more with your life?

Do you feel that you are a burden to your relatives?

Do you have to look after relatives who are a burden?

Do you regularly worry about falling ill?

Do you regularly take medicines you yourself buy from the chemist or drug store?

Do you feel bitter about the way you or a member of your

family has been treated by a doctor?

Do you find advertisements difficult to ignore?

Do you regularly borrow money from non-institutional sources?

Do you change your car regularly because of variations in styling?

Do you take examinations you do not need to take, simply to acquire qualifications?

Do you only enjoy sports when you are competing?

Do you puff and pant if you have to run to catch a bus?

Do you look at your watch a great deal?

Do you smoke?

Do you drink alone regularly?

Do you worry about your weight but do nothing about it?

Do you give up smoking every year?

Do you take sleeping tablets regularly?

Do you need to take tranquillizers regularly?

Do you avoid stairs whenever possible?

Do you drink at work?

Do you dress to please strangers rather than yourself and the people you know?

Do you never take vacations?

Do you find it impossible to relax if you go away for the weekend?

Answer all these questions honestly for cheating helps no one. Each question to which you have answered 'yes' points to a potential source of stress. Sometimes there will be no escape, but acknowledging the problem will often in itself provide some relief. Often there will be a choice and you must decide whether there is anything you can do to protect yourself or whether you are prepared to accept the risk involved.

**Learn to accept some pressures**

Responsibilities, whether at home or at work, add to the quality of life as long as they are kept within reasonable limits. All of us have to accept some anxieties, and life without any worry would be quite tasteless and insipid. To get the most out of life it is necessary to find your optimum pressure level and to live and play hard within that ceiling of pressure without allowing the level of distress to rise to unacceptable limits.

Sometimes, of course, early warning signs are deliberately ignored because the possible advantages which can be gained are sufficiently attractive. For example, a businessman about to conclude a good deal may regard his ulcer as a necessary price to pay for high profits. While we live, most of us must be prepared to face up to a wide variety of stresses. The responsibilities of looking after a family, buying a house and doing a worthwhile job are all likely to produce stresses and strains but they are all nevertheless responsibilities few of us would be prepared to entirely forego. Life without stress would be like beef without mustard, eggs without salt or salad without dressing. It would be dull, tasteless and unappetizing. The man who never knows strain will never know the joy to be obtained from achievement. In a life without stress there can be no relief for pressure and ambition give our lives the mountains of pleasure and the valleys of fear.

## KNOW YOURSELF

To understand how pressures affect you it helps to understand your own motivations and to know a little about the way in which the human mind tries to cope with pressures and problems which may not have elicited a conscious response. Psychoanalysts offer their clients a full breakdown of their psychological make-up in the belief that by understanding themselves people are better able to deal with ordinary day to day problems produced by physical traumas and disordered personal relationships. Although psychoanalysts sometimes take this theory to illogical conclusions there is an element of truth in it. If you understand yourself a little then you are likely to be more self-assured and self-confident. The fact that psychiatrists have a remarkably high suicide rate suggests that a more comprehensive understanding of one's motivations is of very limited value!

**Know your priorities:** We all have ambitions, although modern sociologists and psychologists usually use the word 'goals' instead. Common ambitions are to have good health, to earn lots of money, to obtain a home, to eat well, to have a family, to achieve success, to enjoy sex in plentiful quantities, to acquire lasting friends, to win power and influence and to achieve artistic fulfilment. Obviously different people put their own ambitions in a different order. To know yourself you must have some idea of where your own priorities lie. Acknowledging the fact that priorities exist helps deal with conflicts which inevitably arise. Do not be afraid of admitting your ambitions to yourself and to others. Status and recognition, for example, are common 'goals'.

**How do you get on with other people?**
Our relationships with other people depend very much upon our own attitudes which often vary according to the people with whom we are relating: an aggressive trades union official, for example, may be a kind and sensitive man when dealing with his wife.

There are, however, some simple questions which will help you decide just how well you get on with other people, and just how much they are likely to find you an attractive person.

Are you really interested in them? Even if you aren't interested do you make an effort to pay attention when they are telling you about their new model aeroplane or about how their dog won the inter-collegiate Frisbee catching contest? And do you *look* interested?

Do you admit your own errors or do you always blame others? If you are wrong, do you admit it?

Do you hand out praise more often than criticism? Most people respond better to the carrot than the stick and if criticism is necessary it often helps to wrap it up in a little praise. If the potatoes are undercooked and you feel you must tell the cook, how about some praise for the meat?

Do you think before responding to other people? Many arguments are started because the second person misunderstood what the first person said and responded angrily. Perhaps you could ride with the first punch occasionally.

When you give orders and instructions to subordinates do you do it politely or do you simply snap out the order? It is often possible to get things done speedily and efficiently by suggesting rather than baldly ordering.

## What habits have you got?

Many habits are beneficial but it does help to know what your habits are. For one thing, when existing habits are changed pressures may well be produced. And changes in one sphere of life often precede changes of habit. For example, a man who changes his job may travel to work in a different way. He may therefore no longer pass the shop where he usually buys his newspaper. He may no longer meet his friend at the bus stop.

Habits make chores less of a strain. If you have to actively remember to clean your teeth after a meal then cleaning your teeth is a chore which adds to your accumulation of daily strains. If, however, you clean your teeth automatically after each meal then cleaning your teeth is a useful habit. Without useful habits to help guide us through the day we would have to make far more decisions than we make at the moment. Habits help us to get to work without thinking too much about it and help us keep fed and washed without too much mental effort!

Of course, some ostensibly useful habits may be harmful. If you eat a doughnut every morning simply as a habit and you're trying to lose weight then that is one habit you must get rid of; if you stop off for a drink on the way home then perhaps that too is a habit that you can manage without. Make a list of all your habits and decide which ones are worth holding on to and which ones you could profitably dispense with. Many minor physical habits which are annoying to others and which are done without awareness are a result of pressure. Floor pacing, pencil chewing, tapping fingers, scratching ears, pulling ear lobes, tapping teeth with thumb nail, cracking knuckles, shaking legs, or fiddling with hair or moustache are all gestures used by people under pressure. These are not only annoying to others – they also waste energy.

## HOW DO YOU COPE WITH PROBLEMS?

We all use many different defence mechanisms to help us deal with problems which have arisen from our relationships with other people and the outside world. Here are some of them. You will undoubtedly recognize many of these mechanisms as ones you yourself have used; others you will recognize as commonly used by people you know. These mental tricks are not necessarily dangerous or bad for you.

### Rationalization

A man who has applied for the job of foreman may console himself when he hears that he has been unsuccessful by telling his wife, 'I didn't want the job anyway. It's badly paid and I'd lose the respect of my friends.'

His wife will probably support his feeling if she loves him.

'You're quite right,' she'll nod, 'We're much better-off as we are.'

If she has been pushing him to apply for the job, however, and is now disappointed that he has not been appointed she may quarrel with his new judgement and point out that he did want the job, that it is better paid and that she doesn't care what his friends think.

Used properly, rationalization can be a tremendous asset. The man whose wife supports and strengthens his rationale will eventually feel quite pleased that he didn't get the job. He'll be grateful that he was fortunate enough not to have become a foreman. He'll suffer very little from the fact that he was unlucky in his application. On the other hand, the man whose wife is less comforting will probably suffer more when his carefully devised explanation, designed to fool only himself and her, has been punctured. (Naturally male and female roles are always interchangeable.)

Rationalization is best used as a private defence mechanism unless you can be sure of support from the person with whom you share the rationalization.

### Projection

The woman who cannot cook very well blames her oven. 'How do you expect me to cook you good meals?' she demands of her husband, 'when the cooker is five years old and completely out of date?'

This woman is using the information and advertising material provided by the cooker manufacturers to enable her to project her own inadequacies on to her cooker.

'The bad workman blames his tools,' goes the old saying and that is true of most of us from time to time. The golfer who makes a bad shot will blame his clubs. The company executive who is responsible for an administrative foul up will blame the manager of the minor subsidiary who failed to provide her with the required materials at half a day's notice. The gardener whose seeds don't grow will blame either the seed merchant or the soil.

In all these cases the person involved has projected his or her own failure on to someone else or on to some material object which cannot avoid the blame.

People also project their own feelings on to others. For example, the man whose car breaks down on a lonely road late at night may set off to look for help. He may have no overcoat to protect him from the heavy rain that is falling and there will inevitably be no moon to make up for the fact that the battery in his torch is flat. With so much against him our unfortunate motorist may be forgiven for believing that the world is not treating him fairly. He may assume that even if he finds a farm or a lonely house the occupier is not going to let him use the telephone. 'Would I let a bedraggled stranger in on a night like this?' he may ask himself.

When he does at last find a small lonely cottage the motorist approaches it with severe reservations about the reception he is likely to receive. Before he rings the doorbell he feels certain that he is going to be refused help. He is in a bad mood and he knows that he wouldn't help a complete stranger who arrived soaked and bedraggled on his doorstep.

So when the owner of the cottage, a kindly retired clergyman with a heart of gold, opens the door he is surprised to see an angry man standing there. 'Stuff your telephone,' shouts the motorist, 'I don't want your bloody help.' And with that he turns on his heel and marches away, having projected his own feelings on to the completely innocent and unfortunate clergyman who would, of course, have been perfectly happy to offer food, drink and telephone to a stranded stranger.

This defence mechanism is not usually a wise one to use. It leaves the person who uses it feeling aggrieved and unsatisfied.

**Displacing aggression**

The vice chairman of International Telephone Polishing Services Inc. is told off by the chairman for failing to arrange a deal with South Seas Underground Window Cleaning Services Inc. The vice chairman castigates the managing director for not having provided him with the latest figures from the accounts department on time. Then the managing director ticks off his assistant who snarls at his secretary who shouts at the tea lady who screams at the hall porter who snaps at his wife who scolds their son who kicks the cat who frightens the life out of a poor sparrow. None of these unfortunate folk realize that their problems started when the company's Parisian agent failed to obtain tickets for the Paris Opera on behalf of the company chairman whose wife is a great fan of the Italian soprano, Bella Laudli.

It would have been far less traumatic for all concerned if the chairman had taken his aggression out on a punchball or had chosen to smash a couple of old plates in the stables at his spacious country home! A game of squash or a few minutes in the gym might also have helped ease the chairman's feeling of anger.

We all use this technique of displacing aggression on to other people or on to objects and it has advantages and disadvantages. The main advantage is that the angry person doesn't allow his feelings to build up inside himself: he passes the feeling on to someone or something else. This is much better than simply allowing the feelings of frustration and anger to build up inside for if this happens then the person involved will probably develop a genuine stress disorder. The main disadvantage of course, is that a great many perfectly innocent people may suffer. Some of them may be paid to accept the boss's displaced aggression. Others will neither expect it or be able to cope with it. For this reason it is far better if aggressive feelings are displaced on to inanimate objects such as squash balls, gymnasium floors, running tracks or pieces of faulty and unwanted china. There's a lot to be said for keeping a store of old plates somewhere so that you can smash them when you're feeling uptight. Greeks do a lot of this when they're enjoying themselves in restaurants.

## Nostalgia

The cry, 'The old days were best' is a common one. Many people enjoy music and fashions from past decades because in this way they can hide from modern problems and unwelcome advances. Problems can arise when the past becomes more real than the present for it is impossible to escape from our technological age. Even those who choose to ignore the modern world and live off the land can usually only manage to keep their heads in the sand for a short period. Enjoy the past but don't try to fool yourself that you can ignore the present.

## Specialization

Classically it is university professors who are so lost in their own worlds that they go outside in their carpet slippers, forget to put their ties on, cannot remember where they parked the car and do not know the month or even the year. Many great academic figures have been so wrapped up in their own speciality that they have been quite unable to accept the fact that there is a world outside their own subject.

This is an effective way of closing out the problems of the real world but those who use this mechanism may suffer very badly if their private world collapses or of the problems of the real world become unavoidable. The only people who can use this type of mechanism really effectively are those who have others around them to ensure that the bills are paid and that minor infringements of the law are dealt with painlessly. An academic man whose wife looks after the practical aspects of his life may well be unable to look after himself or to survive at all in the real world after his wife's death.

To a much lesser extent we can all use this defence mechanism to help us lock out the world's problems for short periods of time. Someone whose hobby involves model train building and running may use his hobby to enable him to escape from a stressful world at weekends and during the evenings. Specialist sports followers who enjoy the majestic achievements of their heroes and follow the fortunes of the various teams involved in their sport often manage to escape successfully from the problems of the coal polishing industry or the peanut salting factory (see also hero worship).

## Compensation

The man who is unable to obtain academic success may compensate himself (and those whose love and support he has) by being successful at sports. The man whose business career is less than sparkling may nevertheless achieve success with his hobby.

'Maybe I cannot become chief clerk,' says the clerk seeing his junior promoted above him, 'but my roses are better than anyone else's.'

Similarly, young people who are physically weak or disabled may take to sports which they can do successfully and achieve considerable prestige at them. For example, a young girl who is physically weak may take up swimming and eventually become a champion.

We all need to be successful at something in order to achieve personal satisfaction and to feel wanted. Everyone is good at something and it is essential that we all find out just what we can excel at. To compensate may also be to specialize.

## Hero worship

This enables the young office typist doing a boring job which demands little physically or mentally to share the full and exciting rewarding life of a rock star, fashion model or professional tennis player. Surprisingly, many people who might appear to have satisfying jobs envy others. So the rock star may dream of being a racing motorist and the top jockey may worship the film star he'd like to emulate.

Hero worship is generally a harmless way to escape the duller days of life but the people who enjoy life at first hand rather than at second hand probably achieve more genuine and long-lasting satisfaction.

## Regression

Many modern businessmen have toys on their office desks.

These are often expensively made and well-designed but they are nevertheless toys. They enable the executive to regress to his childhood in moments of crisis but because they are well-made and expensive they do not detract from his image as a successful and wealthy person.

Playing with toys and games helps by taking the executive back to the days when decisions were fairly simple and responsibilities slight. Games can help us all by enabling us to forget our immediate problems and concentrate on less important tasks. Playing solitaire, or playing with a yo-yo can help reduce physical and mental tension at times of crisis. The man or woman who can switch off from major decision making and spend a few minutes with a toy or game will be able to ward off many stress-induced illnesses.

Incidentally, hospital patients often find it comforting to regress to childhood and leave all decisions to the doctors and nurses looking after them. In childhood we know that our parents will solve all major problems and we have a comforting sense of security as a result. This is exactly what the sick often need. They need to trust others and to abdicate normal responsibilities.

### Day-dreaming
We all dream from time to time. It helps in boring or unpleasant moments to drift away to another place. This is a particularly useful defence mechanism. Some people find life so unbearable that they live in a permanent day-dream. Those mental patients who are convinced that they are really Napoleon or Josephine are usually happy enough in their private world. However, day-dreaming can give a false sense of satisfaction. It is important for the dreamer to retain a hold on reality!

### Ideological solutions
The recent popularity of figures such as the Maharishi Yogi shows how quasi-religious solutions are sought by people looking for relief in a new ideology. Similarly, the terrorist organizations which recruit so easily in many different countries

depend for their attraction upon the fact that they offer their converts a way to escape from the other, more trivial, problems of modern living.

### Apathy

Another way to cope with problems very effectively in the short term is to simply ignore them. You don't have to be a drop-out to choose the apathy road. Many people who have regular jobs drop out each evening by slumping down in front of the television set.

These defence mechanisms are not necessarily harmful. Problems arise when they are used subconsciously to such an extent that the user becomes dependent upon one or other of them. When used consciously they may be effective stress dissolutives.

## THE FOUR CORNERSTONES OF LIFE

When the problem areas in your life have been identified and you are deciding what changes you need to make, and which ones can be made without too much disruption, it is important to remember that each person's life has four cornerstones and that if these are damaged or changed too much the quality of life may be irreversibly harmed.

These four cornerstones are: family; work; leisure; friends. When vital changes are being made to the structure of one cornerstone do not make changes to another cornerstone. Do not begin a new job and move house in the same week.

### Happy families

Everyone, rich and poor, royal or common, needs to have a happy family to survive successfully. Domestic peace is an important cornerstone for a happy life.

The basic unit of a family is the two person partnership and if the effects of pressures from the outside world are to be minimized the relationship between the two partners must be a good one. When there is dissent and strife at home the effects of problems originating in the outside world are magnified. A happy home life helps put problems from other areas in perspective.

During recent years there has been considerable pressure from the media for all people to consider sex to be the most important factor in the development and maintenance of a happy marriage. This is nonsense. Not even the most concupiscent and energetic couple could spend more than a small fraction of their waking hours engaged in sexual callisthenics. Eating, bathing, resting, working and other non-sexual activities take up a good deal of any couple's time. A man and a woman who contemplate marriage should, first and foremost, be good friends. In fact the men or women who can marry their best friends are luckiest.

To maintain a stable and happy family each partner must learn to listen as well as to talk, to take and to give, to be courteous and grateful for kindnesses which might easily be taken for granted. Discussing each other's problems is perhaps the most important way that marital partners can help each other. Letting your swain help you take the strain is wise.

## Work
'Work banishes those three great evils: boredom, vice and poverty.' (Voltaire, *Candide*).

Work is not always the cornerstone it should be. Too many people have jobs which they do not enjoy and which serve only to feed them and their family. Workers and trades unions do, however, have the power to improve the quality of routine work by advising employers on methods of organizing tedious tasks so that employees achieve most satisfaction. Much of the distress and frustration suffered by employees working on conveyor belts is caused by a total lack of control over the speed and quality of the work done. Properly organized protests should result in the re-designing of work schedules with greater responsibility being given to workers. Energy and money currently spent by industry on treating the effects of physiological stress could more sensibly be spent on preventing distress.

Ambition is an important driving force for many workers. It must be recognized that failure (even comparative failure) to achieve ambitions may produce distress. Failure is closely linked to ambition and the young man whose parents have high hopes for him may consider himself a failure if he obtains a junior managerial post alongside a man of similar age who has pulled himself up without education or patronage and who quite rightly considers himself a success. To minimize the deleterious effects likely to result ambition needs to be either tempered with common sense or not taken too seriously. If you take your work seriously don't set your sights too high.

We all have the opportunity to make other peoples' work more pleasant and therefore to help reduce the pressures under which others are working. For example, the shopper in a queue who agitates for service when the assistants are working as quickly as they can is increasing the distress suffered by the assistants. Parents who badger schoolteachers and patients who are impatient in the doctor's waiting room also add to the difficulties others have to cope with. Praising people with whom we come into contact when they have provided good service not only makes the recipient feel good – it also makes the person giving the praise feel good. At a garage I patronize the proprietor provides an old-fashioned type of service, handling the pumps himself and even offering to clean dirty windscreens. When congratulated on the service he provides he almost purrs with satisfaction and I always feel good when I leave him.

## Leisure time

The average working week now seems to consist of less than 40 hours. If we assume that 60 hours a week are spent in bed that leaves up to 68 hours a week to spend on other activities. If 14 hours are spent eating, 7 hours on various toilet activities and another 7 on travelling there still remain 40 hours a week for pursuing hobbies and doing 'your own thing'.

Those who spend their leisure time watching television are doing little to help themselves deal with the pressures of living. There are many ways in which those 40 hours can be spent wisely, productively and enjoyably. It is worth noting that the number of hours available for leisure each week is approximately equal to the number of hours available for work.

There are many advantages in using leisure time on creative projects. Many of us have to put up with work that provides little satisfaction and less opportunity for us to achieve success or express our own personalities. Even people in high income jobs often find their work boring and unrewarding. It is, however, much easier to find a satisfying and rewarding leisure time activity which provides an opportunity to achieve success and express an individual personality.

The factory worker who is a member of a team which wins a local sports trophy, the cook whose cakes win prizes, the gardener whose flowers are photographed for the local newspaper, the golfer whose skills win him a low handicap and the photographer whose pictures are displayed in a shop window all find satisfaction and reward from leisure time activity.

There are many forms of leisure activity which in addition to providing participants with respect and personal satisfaction may provide other longer lasting rewards. For example, the man who takes up a sport will become fitter and more able to cope with physical strains. Exercise does not have to involve dull work on machines or in the gymnasium. Cycling, swimming, running, golf and tennis are just a few of the many sporting activities which offer participants both the chance to achieve success and the opportunity to become physically fit. Physically active people also have the advantage that they can take out their anger on the sports ground. Hitting a tennis ball or squash ball is a good alternative to hitting the boss or traffic warden. Incidentally, people who play sports to relax should preferably play alone and not in competition with others. Competitive sports are not suitable for those hoping to rid themselves of tensions; they are, however, ideally suitable for those who are anxious to achieve success and personal satisfaction in some sphere outside their daily work.

Many people spend much of their leisure time on community projects. Sometimes community activities which provide spiritual and physical satisfactions can be found. For example, clearing waste land, reclaiming spoilt countryside and so on are all ways to find both physical and mental satisfaction. Other community activities provide an outlet for purely mental energy. Supporting campaigns fighting local or national government policies provides many with a sense of some power to make their voices heard. This is an excellent antidote to the frustration often engendered by the bureaucratic masters we often seem to serve. It is important, though, to ensure that you do not allow yourself to be given enormous secretarial responsibilities for an Action Committee. It is very easy for potentially satisfying and tension-relieving activities to become frustrating and tension-producing.

Work in the service of any cause you respect is an excellent way to achieve a sense of contentment and fulfilment. Many voluntary workers are altruistic egoists. They volunteer because they themselves benefit as much as those for whom they work. There is absolutely nothing wrong in this. Belief in a religious or moral principle or code of conduct provides such excellent spiritual support that many whose beliefs result in their being persecuted by other segments of society are clearly unscarred, physically or mentally, by quite frightening experiences which, without the feeling of fighting for a just cause as protection, would be permanently damaging. I recently drove past a church outside which there stood a placard reading, 'Jesus is the Lord. Have no anxiety he is near.' Clearly the clergyman who had put that placard in place knew one of the attractions of his cause. (Because of the comfort offered by the common cause many people find wartime surprisingly free of frustration and anxiety.)

Acquiring a pet provides many people with more than just a small mouth to feed. Researchers have shown that elderly people who are lonely and children who are emotionally deprived often benefit when given pet animals to look after. There are often advantages to be obtained from having an animal to take for a walk. For example, a man who buys a dog will have to take it for a walk – and while doing so he'll get exercise he might not otherwise have.

In addition to forty hours a week leisure time most people enjoy approximately four weeks holiday each year. It is important to use those weeks wisely. Holidays are a time for relaxation and a change from normal chores and duties. Many people make the mistake of planning hectic tours which leave them exhausted by the time they return. Some choose self-catering holidays without thinking of the obligations of the cook and bottle washer. It is no holiday for a woman if she is simply exchanging one sink for another. Chores must be shared to minimize their effect. Holidays spent at home can be very relaxing as long as normal routines are ignored.

## The importance of having friends

There is no easy way to define true friendship but I think that most readers would agree with the old adage that a true friend is someone who provides help and support in times of trouble.

Although many books have been written on the subject it does seem to be difficult to define exactly why two people become friends. True friendship depends, I suppose, on some combination of respect and affection. Once real friendships have been forged troubles and pleasures can be shared. A trouble shared may not be halved but it is certainly reduced while a pleasure that cannot be shared is of comparatively little value.

Like the other three cornerstones of life, friendship is vital to the man or woman under stress. And that, of course, is all of us.

## THE VALUES AND LIMITATIONS OF MEDICAL INTERVENTION

Fear and anxiety, distress and confusion, frustration and insecurity; these are the causes of more illness than all the bacteria and viruses in the developed world where most of the major infectious diseases have been controlled by antibiotics, vaccines and public health measures.

Preventive medicine is usually regarded by members of the medical profession as something of an afterthought, an ancillary to the main function of medicine which is making ill people healthy. When it comes to dealing with infectious diseases, however, governments have been careful to ensure that some genuine effort is made to prevent the spread of disease. The interest in infective disorder being inspired largely by the fact that these diseases are likely to spread within a whole community. An epidemic of smallpox could completely alter a nation's economic status. Stress diseases on the other hand are not communicated from one sufferer to another healthy citizen. They affect only one person at a time, consequently governments have had little interest in preventing their development.

Nor has the medical profession been very quick to try to prevent stress diseases. Doctors are traditionally more interested in treating disease than in preventing the development of disease. After all, it is usual for doctors to be paid to help heal a sick person rather than to keep a fit person healthy. The ancient Chinese were the exceptions; they paid their physicians when they were well and stopped paying them when they felt ill. Doctors, and hence medical researchers, are therefore more interested in treating a sick person than in keeping a healthy one healthy, although it would surely be more sensible for a doctor to pick up a broom handle he sees lying in the street than to keep treating the people who break their legs on it.

The only real concession that the medical profession has made to the growing range of stress diseases is to offer a wider variety of palliative therapies and symptomatic treatments. Apart from offering treatment for physical symptoms resulting from the effects of pressure on the body, doctors offer several varieties of treatment for the mental symptoms exhibited by the distressed. These remedies may also be offered to patients with purely physical symptoms when the observing physician decides that the physical symptoms may be a result of psychological strains. According to his personal inclinations a doctor may suggest that his distressed patient talks about his problems, takes drugs or has an operation. In the following sections I describe the dubious advantages of these remedies.

What doctors rarely suggest is that their patients prepare themselves for times of trouble. Such actions would, of course, hardly be popular in the medical profession. It would, after all, result in the loss of a considerable amount of work for members of the profession. In later sections of this book I explain how you can best look after yourself and prevent the development of stress diseases.

## Psychotherapy

Some psychotherapists argue that just as symptoms such as fever, headache and joint pains are indicative of an underlying virus infection, so depression, anxiety and other symptoms of neurotic behaviour are merely indicative of an underlying mental complex. They argue that just as physicians attempt to treat the cause of a patient's symptoms rather than the symptoms themselves, so it should be the neurotic's complex which is treated rather than his symptoms. Psychiatrists spend many hours with their patients trying to unravel these complexes. They spend weeks, months, and if the patient has sufficient cash, years searching for hidden feelings, desires and frustrations and then helping the patient understand and conquer those feelings. Unfortunately there is little evidence to suggest that psychiatrists do any good at all. Indeed, no two psychiatrists agree on exactly how to search for those hidden feelings and no two agree on the best ways to treat whatever it is they think they have uncovered.

Behavioural psychologists believe that there is no need to treat underlying complexes but that the symptoms are all that need attention. They argue that the neurotic symptoms are simply conditioned responses which result from faulty learning processes. In other words, neurotics are made not born. To remove the symptoms behavioural psychologists claim that all that is necessary is a type of re-education – the patient must learn to react in a different way to the situations and problems which are responsible for his symptoms. He must adjust his behaviour.

Behavioural psychologists have a great deal of success with some patients. Agorophobics, for example, are afraid to step outside the house. There is usually some reason, often long forgotten, sometimes never understood, for this fear. The behavioural psychologists argue that all the patient has to do is learn how to go outside again. It must be done slowly and gradually, by taking a couple of steps outside and then slowly day by day, moving further and further away from the safety and security of the house. To cure people frightened of cats it is said to be simply necessary to get the sufferer used to cats. The patient begins by looking at photographs, moves on to stroking simulated cat fur, watches other people touching cats and then does the same himself. The patient with an excessive fear of authority must learn to think of authoritarian figures as simple and clay-footed human beings who bathe, defecate and sleep like the rest of us.

For those patients who have specific problems and fears behaviour therapy can be most effective. The patient has simply to re-educate himself. Unfortunately, most people do not have specific fears. Their problems and difficulties are widely based. They suffer because of problems at work, strains at home, crises on the roads and difficulties in their personal relationships. There is no simple, single threat for them to overcome.

**Brain surgery**
Since the 1930s surgeons have been cutting out little bits of human brain in attempts to repair the disordered workings of their patients' minds. Walter Freeman, a Professor of Neurology at Washington University was a great advocate of this type of surgery. During the ten years from 1940 to 1950 he wrote fifty-six articles extolling the virtues of neurosurgery and himself did some 4,000 operations. In 1971 the British Medical Journal estimated that a total of about 100,000 operations had been done on human brains by surgeons seeking to control mentally disordered patients.

Operations involving either cutting away or simply damaging parts of the brain have been done on patients with depression, obsessional neurosis, anxiety states, hysteria, eczema, asthma, anorexia nervosa, ulcerative colitis, hypertension, and angina. All of these conditions can, of course, be either caused, or made worse by problems and pressures.

There has for some time been a huge controversy within the medical profession about the value of operations of this kind. Most thinking doctors believe that it is wrong to deliberately destroy part of a patient's brain without there being any evidence to show that such destructive operations are helpful. The surgeons and psychiatrists who advocate the operation argue that afterwards their patients are calmer and uncomplaining. Since patients who have had operations of this kind are usually rather zombie-like it is hardly surprising that they do not complain much! To argue that this proves that surgery on the brain is effective is rather like arguing that ripping the insides out of a television is a good way to deal with distortion and interference. Most wise people would find looking at a blank screen unsatisfying.

Destructive psychosurgery is not the only way in which surgeons claim to be able to help people under pressure. A rather more subtle form of control is offered by surgeons who practise electronic stimulation of the brain. This practice depends on mapping out the sites within the brain where various categories of thought and emotion originate. Instead of simply destroying part of the brain he thinks to be functioning faultily the surgeon inserts electrodes, fits terminals on to the scalp and then passes small quantities of electrical current along the wires. Receivers can be fitted on to the scalp so that electrical impulses can be fired into the brain from some distance away. The receivers fit under wigs or hats and are supplied with long-lasting batteries.

With his electrodes in position (and remember that all this is happening – this is not science fiction) the patient can be controlled quite effectively. He can be made to eat, to sleep or to work. His appetite, heart rate, body temperature and other factors can also be controlled. Patients stimulated in the right place can be persuaded to stop eating or to start flirting and talking about nothing but sex. One doctor has fitted epileptic patients with electrodes and transmitters, another physician predicts that patients requiring anaesthesia will in future be put to sleep with the aid of electrodes in their brains.

The doyen of these researchers is Dr Delgado of Yale University School of Medicine. In one particularly dramatic experiment Dr Delgado wired a bull with electrodes and then planted himself in the middle of a bullring with a cape and a small radio transmitter. The bull charged but was stopped by Dr Delgado pressing a button on his transmitter, the bull screeching to a halt inches away from its target. Dr Delgado has reported that, 'animals with implanted electrodes in their brains have been made to perform a variety of responses with predictable reliability as if they were electronic toys under human control.'

## Drugs

About one fifth of all the prescriptions given to patients in America, the United Kingdom and most other Western countries are for sleeping pills, tranquillizers and anti-depressants. Valium, a well-known tranquillizer made by Roche, the massive Swiss company, is the best-selling prescribed drug in both America and the United Kingdom. In England, for example, out of a total of some 350 million prescriptions signed every year about 75 million prescriptions are for drugs which have an effect on the nervous system. The market for these drugs, given to patients who cannot sleep, who are anxious or who cannot relax properly is growing rapidly and the world's major drug companies are all anxiously producing new variations on existing themes to compete with the hold that Roche have over the market. When you remember that pressure is a direct cause of many other common and persistent problems such as hypertension, indigestion and angina you will see just how much money drug companies are making out of stress-induced illnesses.

The biggest international addiction problem is not teenagers taking hash but middle-agers taking tranquillizers. It has been said that if all the people on tranquillizers were banned from driving or operating machinery (as they should be) the world's economy would collapse overnight. The pill-taking habit usually starts at some time of genuine crisis. A close friend or relative has died, there is a rush on at work to get a special and important job finished, there are examinations to be taken and so on. All these problems may precipitate a visit to the doctor and the prescribing of the inevitable relaxant. Pills may prove helpful during those early dark days. The real danger is that after the darkest days are over when the gloom is a little less impenetrable the pill taking will continue. It is much easier to start taking pills than it is to stop taking them.

**Some of the drugs most commonly prescribed**

*Amphetamines*: Amphetamines became popular as pep pills after it became known that people who take them feel physically and mentally fresh and active while depressions and lethargies disappear under their influence. First synthesized in Los Angeles in 1927 amphetamine has been a controversial drug since it was reported in 1938 that people may become addicted to it. The medical profession found it difficult to decide for many years whether or not the drug was harmful. In 1954 the Chief Medical Officer at the Ministry of Health in Britain described amphetamines as non-toxic, without serious side effects and non-addictive, but in 1966 the American Food and Drug Administration estimated that over twenty-five tons (half the annual domestic production) of amphetamine found its way into illegal channels – enough to provide everyone in America with fourteen tablets a year. It was estimated that year that in Oklahoma City (population 300,000) there were 5,000 addicts.

Today it is well accepted that amphetamines are such dangerous drugs that their use is never justified. Most respectable doctors no longer prescribe amphetamines but there is still a black market.

*Barbiturates*: Barbituric acid was first prepared in 1864 by a twenty-nine year old research chemist called Adolph von Baeyer who was then a chemist in Ghent. He is said to have celebrated his discovery by visiting a pub which was full of officers celebrating St Barbara's Day, and that was how the drug got its name. Since then more than 25,000 barbiturates have been produced and about 50 marketed for use. The drugs are usually given to help sedate worried or nervous people and to help people who have trouble getting off to sleep. There is no doubt that the barbiturates are effective.

Unfortunately they do cause problems. Barbiturates kill about 10,000 people a year in the United States. There are 500,000 regular users in the United Kingdom obtaining their supplies quite legally from doctors. Many of these people have exactly the same mental problems as they had when they started taking barbiturates but in addition they now have their barbiturate addiction to contend with. As long ago as 1950 the addiction of patients to barbiturates was described as being more serious than the addiction of people to morphine. In that year at the United States Public Health Service Addiction Research Centre at Lexington, Kentucky, five volunteers were given barbiturates for three months. When the barbiturates were withdrawn all five volunteers suffered severe mental illnesses and had epileptic fits.

Barbiturates are commonly used by people wishing to commit suicide (see pp. 191-194). They are effective for this purpose: three people a day die from deliberate barbiturate overdosage in the United Kingdom. Barbiturates also cause a deterioration in the personality of the person taking them which is so serious that one psychiatrist has made quite a name for himself in treating forgetful and confused people in their later years. He simply takes them off their barbiturate tablets.

*Valium, Librium and the other benzodiazepines*: Valium is one of the international best selling drugs of all time. Librium, its sister drug, is also a regular top ten hit, as is Mogadon, also a Roche product and a close relative of the two big sellers. A fourth superdrug, Nobrium, introduced in 1971 with a tremendous fanfare of glowing publicity has been far less successful. Other companies also make drugs which are members of the same group and which are sometimes identical in chemical composition to Valium and the other Roche products but these look-alike products take only a relatively small part of this particular market.

All these drugs tend to calm the anxious and relax the tensed. There are unfortunate side effects with them. It has been shown that people who have taken a benzodiazepine and who stop the drug sometimes show withdrawal symptoms. Mild symptoms include tremor, agitation, headache and nausea. In more serious cases there is considerably greater difficulty. In October 1977 the *Drug and Therapeutics Bulletin* pointed out that physical dependence can occur with these drugs and a report from the Kansas University Medical Centre showed that patients who suddenly stop taking them may become psychotic.

There are hazards when pregnant women take pills. When taken during the third month of pregnancy benzodiazepines may cause babies to be born deformed. This is particularly frightening when one realizes that a survey of 156 pregnant American women showed that about a quarter had taken an antidepressant during pregnancy. Benzodiazepines are excreted in breast milk with a resulting blood level in infants of approximately one half to two third of the adult level.

*Meprobamate*: Meprobamate was introduced in the early 1950s as a safe replacement for the barbiturates. In 1956 it was shown to cause allergy reactions and to be no-more effective than sugar pills in helping people cope with anxiety. It was, however, found that people who took it sometimes became physically dependent upon it. It was prescribed widely under the trade names Miltown in the United States and Equanil in the United Kingdom and is still widely used although a number of experts now believe that it does no real good at all and may do harm. People who rely on this drug would probably be better off taking chocolate beans.

**Self-prescribed solutions;**
*Alcohol and tobacco*: Alcohol and tobacco are two stress dissolutives commonly employed by people under pressure who are looking for short-term solutions. The disadvantages of these two remedies are discussed on pages 119 and 87 respectively. Many patients who develop cancer of the lung or cirrhosis of the liver are indirectly victims of anxiety: their own solutions have done the damage. It is often said that about half of all illnesses have a direct psychological basis. It is equally true to say that about one half of the remainder are caused by remedies (such as drinking and smoking) applied by patients themselves. It is not only the treatments prescribed by doctors which can prove harmful.


## STRESS-PROOF YOUR BODY

If you buy any piece of expensive equipment you will probably protect it from the elements when you can, feed it the right fuels and have it repaired and serviced whenever necessary. You'll probably want to learn a little about how it works and how to deal with minor faults. Such good care will undoubtedly pay dividends. The machine will start when you want it to, will run smoothly and reliably and breakdowns will be infrequent. Like any other machine the human body works best when looked after. And since the body you've got is, barring major transplant surgery developments, the only one you're ever likely to get, it is wise to look after it.

Do everything you can to improve your general state of health. In a fit and healthy body it is far easier to avoid the harmful effects of strain. The firmly built and well-maintained structure lasts longer under seige than the frail and disordered edifice. Most of us can improve the state of our bodies and our resistance to strain by reducing our weight and taking up light exercise. The overweight man puts an extra strain on his bodily organs before he starts doing anything energetic. The flabby and out of condition person is far less able to cope with any change in the immediate environment. Eating the correct amount of the right foods is vital.

It is also sensible to learn how to look after yourself and others in your family when you or they have contracted minor illnesses. You don't have to spend hours at evening classes learning how to rewrap Tutankhamen unless you want to but you can easily and quickly learn how to prepare yourself for emergencies. Buy a good, simply written first aid book and keep it handy in the kitchen. Buy a few simple remedies and keep them in a locked cupboard ready for emergencies but out of reach of children. You should try to cope with minor problems yourself; if you are always calling the doctor for advice he'll be less inclined to believe that you really are in trouble when you genuinely need urgent help.

People who suffer from chronic illnesses should contact one of the many organizations which exist to help people with specific illnesses. For example, there are organizations run by diabetics for diabetics. Patients newly found to have this disease can learn about the disease and how to conquer some of the problems by associating with fellow sufferers. Help, support and reassurance are available from many hundreds of organizations around the world. Your doctor should be able to put you in touch with the relevant address. If he can't help try the local library.

**Dieting — girth control**

The accompanying table should give you an idea of whether or not you are overweight. You were probably at your ideal weight at the age of twenty. I'm afraid that you cannot explain away extra weight by simply arguing that you have large bones. This argument is rather comforting but not very convincing. A large-boned person has probably no more than seven pounds of bone more than a small-boned person.

Maximum weights. Heights are measured without shoes, weights are measured with indoor clothing only. These are maximum weights: you should weigh less. If you weigh more then you are fat.

| MEN | | WOMEN | |
|-----|-----|-------|-----|
| Height | Weight | Height | Weight |
| 5′ 2″ | 140 lb | 4′ 11″ | 125 lb |
| 5′ 3″ | 142 lb | 5′ 0″ | 127 lb |
| 5′ 4″ | 147 lb | 5′ 1″ | 129 lb |
| 5′ 5″ | 151 lb | 5′ 2″ | 133 lb |
| 5′ 6″ | 155 lb | 5′ 3″ | 136 lb |
| 5′ 7″ | 160 lb | 5′ 4″ | 140 lb |
| 5′ 8″ | 164 lb | 5′ 5″ | 143 lb |
| 5′ 9″ | 168 lb | 5′ 6″ | 148 lb |
| 5′ 10″ | 173 lb | 5′ 7″ | 152 lb |
| 5′ 11″ | 178 lb | 5′ 8″ | 156 lb |
| 6′ 0″ | 183 lb | 5′ 9″ | 160 lb |
| 6′ 1″ | 188 lb | 5′ 10″ | 164 lb |
| 6′ 2″ | 194 lb | 5′ 11″ | 167 lb |
| 6′ 3″ | 200 lb | | |

When you have decided just how much weight you need to lose start planning how you're going to do it. It is important to remember that the fat you want to get rid of has been put on over the last few years. Each pound of fat in your body represents an excess food intake of about 3,500 calories. If you eat just 50 calories a day more than you need you will put on 5 pounds by the end of a year. If you keep doing this for ten years you will have put on an extra 50 pounds by the end of that time.

So a woman who weighed a modest 100 pounds at 20 years of age could weight 150 pounds at 30 years of age without ever having suddenly put on any excess weight or been guilty of regular eating orgies.

To simply STOP putting on weight you must reduce your diet so that it provides precisely the right number of calories for you. An average housewife who weighs 140 pounds will use up about 2,500 calories a day in breathing, walking, sleeping and washing up. An average businessman who weighs 150 pounds will use up about 3,000 calories a day. To remain the weight they are the housewife must eat 2,500 calories a day and the businessman must not consume more than 3,000 calories a day.

To LOSE weight you must eat less calories than you need each day. If you do that you'll use up stored fat to provide energy.

When you've decided how much weight you want to lose you must decide how fast you want to lose it. Remember that to lose one pound in weight you have got to eat 3,500 calories less than usual. This means that it is far better to plan to lose your excess weight over a period of six months or even a year than to try and lose it all in a few weeks. If you reduce your daily calorie intake by 150 calories you should have lost 14 pounds by the end of a year. That is far more practical than trying to lose 14 pounds in a month. To do that you would have to reduce your daily calorie intake by nearly 2,000 calories.

Here then is the counterstress diet plan:
1. Weigh yourself and decide how much weight you want to lose.
2. Decide how quickly you want to lose that weight. Remember that it is far better to lose weight slowly and regularly than to try to lose enormous quantities of weight overnight.
3. Count your daily calorie intake for a week before you start the diet. Divide by 7 to find your average daily intake. At the end of the week weigh yourself again.
4. If you have put on weight during the week you have been eating more than you need for the work your body does. Every pound you have put on represents an excess of 3,500 calories. If

you have put on 3 pounds then you have eaten 10,500 calories too many during the week.

5. Before you plan your reducing diet you must reduce your daily intake of food to a level at which your weight will remain stable. If you've put on one pound in the week you must reduce your daily intake by 500 calories (one seventh of 3,500 calories).

6. For every extra pound you want to lose you have to reduce intake of calories by 3,500. That means that if you want to lose ten pounds you have to reduce your diet by a total of 35,000 calories. You can either do that by reducing your daily diet by one thousand calories for a month or by reducing your diet by 100 calories for about a year. The end result should be the same. It is obviously easier to reduce by 100 calories a day for a year. And if it's easier you're more likely to stick to the diet.

7. Once you've got down to your ideal weight you can push your daily intake of calories back up to the level at which your weight remains stable. If when you start eating more your weight goes up again then your daily calorie consumption is too high. Remember that an extra 10 calories a day will put on about a pound in a year.

## Other ways of losing weight

Just as instant wealth is a universal dream so is instant svelte.

There are many firms selling slimming aids by post which claim to help the overweight cast off excess pounds. There are companies selling hormones for slimmers and there are doctors who prescribe special slimming tablets or who perform weight-reducing operations on wealthy patients. None of these methods are as effective or as safe as simply eating less. And if you eat less and re-educate your appetite you will solve your problem permanently. You won't need to go running back for more 'help' in another three months' time when you've rebuilt the rolls of fat that the surgeons had so painstakingly removed.

There are many advantages to taking up exercise. Losing weight is not, however, one of them, although persistent energetic exercise does increase the rate at which stored fat deposits are burnt up and does strengthen the muscles so that you'll look thinner even if you're not. Exercise won't help you lose much weight because to get rid of 3,500 calories (the equivalent of one pound of fat) you have to do a great deal of exercise. Arnold Palmer has played a fair amount of golf over the past few years but not even his greatest fans would describe him as slender.

An enthusiastic and determined slimmer who weighs about ten stones and who spends an hour walking or playing golf will use up about 200 calories. A tennis player or jogger will use up about 300 calories and a swimmer, cyclist, rower or runner will use up 400 or 500 calories an hour. (An athlete rowing, cycling or swimming at top speed will naturally use up many more calories than an athlete taking part in a medium or long distance event but the athlete at top speed is extremely unlikely to keep this up for an hour!)

The precise number of calories lost depends on two things: the size of the slimmer and the enthusiasm with which the exercise is done. A twelve stone woman uses up more calories when playing tennis than a six stone woman, just as a Rolls Royce uses up more petrol than a mini car. And a racing cyclist who maintains an average speed of twenty miles per hour for a whole hour will obviously use up more calories than a cyclist who stops for a rest and a chat every hundred yards.

From the list above you can see that a slimmer who walks for half an hour per day will use up about 100 calories a day. Allowing for occasional days in bed with sore feet she could lose ten pounds in a year. A total of 14 hours jogging spread over a week will result in the loss of only one pound of fat. Swimming flat out for over an hour a day will result in a similar weight loss. To lose ten pounds in a week you would have to cycle flat out for 80-90 hours. At twenty miles an hour that would take you nearly 1,800 miles.

And, of course, there is an extra snag. Exercise makes most of us feel hungry. And a cheese sandwich eaten after a game of squash will put back on every calorie that has been used up. Walking for half an hour gives most people a healthy but calorie hungry appetite.

**Counting your calories**

Use a notebook to help you keep a record of the calories you consume. For example:

| | | |
|---|---|---:|
| Breakfast | 1 boiled egg | 90 |
| | Bowl of cereal | 100 |
| | Milk and sugar on cereal | 100 |
| | Cup of black coffee | 5 |
| Snack | Cup of black coffee | 5 |
| | Apple | 60 |
| Mid-day meal | Cheese | 120 |
| | Two slices bread | 140 |
| | Soup (clear) | 40 |
| | ¼ oz of butter (100gm) | 55 |
| | Orange | 50 |
| | Glass of white wine (dry) | 80 |
| Snack | Cup of black coffee | 5 |
| Evening meal | Hamburger | 310 |
| | Chips | 260 |
| | Peas | 35 |
| | Glass of red wine (dry) | 80 |
| | Black coffee | 5 |
| | Ice cream | 110 |
| | Total calories | 1650 |

The figures on this list of calories are inevitably approximates but they do help you to see which foods are most likely to cause an increase in weight. (For example, fresh fruits are clearly less fattening than tinned fruits.) Used sensibly and honestly the list will enable you to count your calories quickly and with acceptable accuracy. Only the most dedicated will weigh all their food meticulously. The rest of us can benefit from simply knowing which foods to avoid whenever possible and from keeping a rough calorie count while actually trying to lose weight. An ounce has been converted to 25 grams so as to give round numbers, though to be exact it is equal to slightly more than that.

| Food | Weight (average helping) | | Calories |
|------|------|------|------|
| Apple | 4oz | 100gm | 60 |
| apple (baked) | 4oz | 100gm | 40 |
| apple crumble | 3oz | 75gm | 200 |
| apple dumpling | 6oz | 150gm | 345 |
| apple sauce | 1oz | 25gm | 20 |
| apricots (fresh) | 3oz | 75gm | 25 |
| apricots (tinned) | 4oz | 100gm | 105 |
| | | | |
| Bacon (grilled) | 2oz | 50gm | 220 |
| bacon (fried) | 2oz | 50gm | 260 |
| banana | 3oz | 75gm | 65 |
| beans (baked) | 5oz | 125gm | 140 |
| beans (french) | 4oz | 100gm | 10 |
| beans (kidney) | 4oz | 100gm | 10 |
| beans (runner) | 4oz | 100gm | 10 |
| beans (broad) | 4oz | 100gm | 50 |
| beans (butter) | 4oz | 100gm | 105 |
| beef (boiled) | 2oz | 50gm | 165 |
| beef (roast) | 2oz | 50gm | 160 |
| beefburger | 4oz | 100gm | 415 |
| beef (corned) | 2oz | 50gm | 130 |
| beef (minced) | 2oz | 50gm | 120 |
| beefsteak (grilled) | 6oz | 150gm | 345 |
| beef stew | 6oz | 150gm | 250 |
| beetroot (boiled) | 2oz | 50gm | 25 |
| biscuits (chocolate) | 2oz | 50gm | 270 |
| biscuits (plain) | 2oz | 50gm | 120 |
| biscuits (sweet) | 2oz | 50gm | 160 |
| blackberries (fresh) | 4oz | 100gm | 30 |
| blackberries (tinned) | 2oz | 50gm | 55 |
| blackcurrants | 3oz | 75gm | 25 |
| black pudding | 3oz | 75gm | 200 |
| blancmange | 4oz | 100gm | 140 |
| brawn | 2oz | 50gm | 160 |
| bread (one slice) | 1oz | 25gm | 70 |
| bread (fried) | 1oz | 25gm | 170 |
| bread sauce | 1oz | 25gm | 30 |

| Food | Weight (average helpings) | | Calories |
|---|---|---|---|
| broccoli | 4oz | 100gm | 15 |
| brussels sprouts | 3oz | 75gm | 15 |
| butter | 1oz | 25gm | 220 |
| Cabbage | 4oz | 100gm | 10 |
| cake (plain) | 2oz | 50gm | 150 |
| cake (rich or iced) | 2oz | 50gm | 210 |
| carrots | 3oz | 75gm | 15 |
| cauliflower | 4oz | 100gm | 15 |
| celery | 3oz | 75gm | 10 |
| cereals | 1oz | 25gm | 100 |
| cheese | 1oz | 25gm average | 120 |
| cheese omelette (one egg) | | | 335 |
| cherries (fresh) | 4oz | 100gm | 50 |
| cherries (glacé) | 1oz | 25gm | 60 |
| chicken (roast) | 3oz | 75gm | 170 |
| chicken (boiled) | 3oz | 75gm | 180 |
| chips | 4oz | 100gm | 260 |
| chocolate | 1oz | 25gm | 160 |
| christmas pudding | 4oz | 110gm | 360 |
| cocoa | 1 cup (made with milk) | | 160 |
| coconut (fresh) | 1oz | 25gm | 105 |
| coconut (desiccated) | 1oz | 25gm | 180 |
| cod (fried) | 6oz | 150gm | 420 |
| cod (steamed) | 6oz | 150gm | 140 |
| coffee (black) | 1 cup | | 5 |
| coffee (white) | 1 cup | | 25 |
| coffee (white and sugar) | 1 cup | | 55 |
| cornflour | 1oz | 25gm | 100 |
| cottage pie | 4oz | 100gm | 120 |
| crab | 3oz | 75gm | 120 |
| cranberries (fresh) | 2oz | 50gm | 10 |
| cream (single) | 1oz | 25gm | 60 |
| cream (double) | 1oz | 25gm | 130 |
| cress | 1oz | 25gm | 4 |
| crisps | 1oz | 25gm | 160 |
| cucumber | 2oz | 50gm | 6 |
| custard | 2oz | 50gm | 75 |

71

| Food | Weight (average helping) | | Calories |
|------|------|------|------|
| Damsons (stewed, fresh) | 4oz | 100gm | 45 |
| damsons (tinned) | 4oz | 100gm | 120 |
| dates | 1oz | 25gm | 60 |
| duck (roast) | 2oz | 50gm | 190 |
| Eggs (boiled) | 1 egg | | 90 |
| eggs (fried) | 1 egg | | 140 |
| egg (poached) | 1 egg | | 90 |
| egg (scrambled) | 1 egg | | 180 |
| Fat (cooking) | 1oz | 25gm | 260 |
| figs (dried) | 1oz | 25gm | 60 |
| fish cake (fried) | 2 cakes | | 250 |
| fish paste | 1oz | 25gm | 35 |
| fruit salad (fresh) | 4oz | 100gm | 80 |
| fruit salad (tinned) | 4oz | 100gm | 100 |
| fruit tart | 3oz | 75gm | 200 |
| fudge | 2oz | 50gm | 180 |
| Glucose | 1oz | 25gm | 100 |
| goose (roast) | 2oz | 50gm | 185 |
| gooseberries (fresh) | 4oz | 100gm | 35 |
| gooseberries (tinned) | 3oz | 75gm | 50 |
| grapefruit (fresh) | 4oz | 100gm | 25 |
| grapefruit (tinned) | 3oz | 75gm | 60 |
| grapes | 4oz | 100gm | 80 |
| gravy (thick) | 1oz | 25gm | 40 |
| gravy (thin) | 1oz | 25gm | 10 |
| greengages (fresh) | 5oz | 125gm | 70 |
| Haddock (fried) | 6oz | 150gm | 400 |
| haddock (steamed) | 6oz | 150gm | 180 |
| halibut (fried) | 6oz | 150gm | 500 |
| halibut (steamed) | 6oz | 150gm | 200 |
| hake (fried) | 6oz | 150gm | 360 |
| hake (steamed) | 6oz | 150gm | 180 |
| ham (grilled) | 6oz | 150gm | 360 |
| ham (boiled) | 2oz | 50gm | 125 |

| Food | Weight (average helping) | | Calories |
|---|---|---|---|
| hamburger (fried) | 3oz | 75gm | 310 |
| hare (casserole) | 4oz | 100gm | 220 |
| heart | 3oz | 75gm | 115 |
| herring (baked) | 4oz | 100gm | 230 |
| herring (fried) | 6oz | 150gm | 400 |
| honey | 1oz | 25gm | 80 |
| Ice cream (vanilla) | 2oz | 50gm | 110 |
| Jam | 1oz | 25gm | 80 |
| jam tart | 1½oz | 40gm | 165 |
| jelly | 4oz | 100gm | 90 |
| Kale | 4oz | 100gm | 45 |
| kidneys (fried) | 3oz | 75gm | 180 |
| kidneys (stewed) | 3oz | 75gm | 135 |
| kipper fillets | 4oz | 100gm | 235 |
| Lamb chop | 5oz | 125gm | 240 |
| lamb (roast) | 2oz | 50gm | 165 |
| lard | 1oz | 25gm | 260 |
| leeks (boiled) | 4oz | 100gm | 30 |
| lemon | 4oz | 100gm | 15 |
| lemon curd | 1oz | 25gm | 80 |
| lentils | 1oz | 25gm | 85 |
| lettuce | 2oz | 50gm | 5 |
| liver (ox, fried) | 4oz | 100gm | 325 |
| liver (pig, fried) | 4oz | 100gm | 200 |
| lobster (boiled) | 3oz | 75gm | 100 |
| loganberries (fresh) | 4oz | 100gm | 20 |
| loganberries (tinned) | 4oz | 100gm | 115 |
| luncheon meat | 2oz | 50gm | 160 |
| Macaroni (dried) | 1oz | 25gm | 105 |
| macaroni (boiled) | 4oz | 100gm | 130 |
| mackerel (fried) | 6oz | 150gm | 210 |
| malted drinks | ½ pint | | 200 |
| mandarin oranges (tinned) | 4oz | 100gm | 70 |

| Food | Weight (average helping) | | Calories |
|---|---|---|---|
| margarine | 1oz | 25gm | 220 |
| marmalade | 1oz | 25gm | 70 |
| marrow | 8oz | 200gm | 15 |
| mayonnaise | 1oz | 25gm | 100 |
| meat paste | 1oz | 25gm | 60 |
| melon (honeydew) | 3oz | 75gm | 35 |
| melon (cantaloupe) | 4oz | 100gm | 16 |
| milk (fresh) | 1oz | 25gm | 20 |
| milk (condensed) | 1oz | 25gm | 100 |
| milk (evaporated) | 1oz | 25gm | 45 |
| milk (skimmed, dried) | 1oz | 25gm | 100 |
| minerals (soft drinks) | 12oz | 300gm | 100 |
| mushrooms (raw) | 1oz | 25gm | 2 |
| mushrooms (fried) | 2oz | 50gm | 125 |
| mutton (roast) | 2oz | 50gm | 175 |
| mutton (boiled) | 2oz | 50gm | 150 |
| mutton (stew) | 4oz | 100gm | 230 |
| | | | |
| Oatmeal (raw) | 1oz | 25gm | 110 |
| oil (cooking | 1oz | 25gm | 260 |
| olives | 3 olives | | 15 |
| onions (boiled) | 3oz | 75gm | 15 |
| onions (spring) | 2oz | 50gm | 20 |
| orange (fresh) | 5oz | 125gm | 50 |
| ox tongue | 2oz | 50gm | 175 |
| oysters (raw) | 6 oysters | | 45 |
| | | | |
| Pancake | 2oz | 50gm | 170 |
| parsnips (boiled) | 4oz | 100gm | 65 |
| parsley (fresh) | 1oz | 25gm | 5 |
| pastry (flaky) | 2oz | 50gm | 265 |
| peaches (fresh) | 4oz | 100gm | 45 |
| peaches (tinned) | 3oz | 75gm | 60 |
| peanuts (roasted) | 1oz | 25gm | 170 |
| pears (fresh) | 6oz | 150gm | 55 |
| pears (tinned) | 2oz | 50gm | 80 |
| peas (fresh) | 2oz | 50gm | 35 |

74

| Food | Weight (average helping) | | Calories |
|------|------|------|------|
| peas (tinned) | 2oz | 50gm | 45 |
| peppers (green) | 1 pepper | | 30 |
| pheasant (roast) | 2oz | 50gm | 120 |
| pickles (not thickened) | 1oz | 25gm | 5 |
| pilchards (tinned) | 4oz | 110gm | 215 |
| pineapple (fresh) | 4oz | 110gm | 40 |
| pineapple (tinned) | 4oz | 110gm | 85 |
| plaice fillets (steamed) | 6oz | 150gm | 150 |
| plaice fillets (fried) | 6oz | 150gm | 360 |
| plums (fresh) | 3oz | 75gm | 35 |
| plums (tinned) | 4oz | 110gm | 90 |
| pork chop (grilled) | 5oz | 125gm | 300 |
| pork (roast) | 2oz | 50gm | 180 |
| popcorn | 2oz | 50gm | 220 |
| porridge (no milk/sugar) | 4oz | 100gm | 55 |
| potatoes (baked) | 4oz | 100gm | 120 |
| potatoes (boiled) | 4oz | 100gm | 95 |
| potatoes (roasted) | 4oz | 100gm | 220 |
| prawns (boiled) | 2oz | 50gm | 60 |
| prunes (cooked and sweet) | 4oz | 100gm | 120 |
| Rabbit (stewed) | 4oz | 100gm | 205 |
| radishes | 2oz | 50gm | 10 |
| raisins | 2oz | 50gm | 140 |
| raspberries (fresh) | 4oz | 100gm | 30 |
| raspberries (tinned) | 4oz | 100gm | 130 |
| redcurrants (fresh) | 4oz | 100gm | 25 |
| rhubarb (fresh) | 4oz | 100gm | 10 |
| rhubarb (stewed and sweet) | 4oz | 100gm | 65 |
| rice (dry) | 1oz | 25gm | 100 |
| rice (boiled) | 4oz | 100gm | 140 |
| rice (pudding) | 4oz | 100gm | 160 |
| roe (fried) | 3oz | 75gm | 225 |
| Sago (dry) | 1oz | 25gm | 100 |
| sago pudding | 4oz | 100gm | 160 |
| salad oil | 1oz | 25gm | 265 |
| salmon (fresh, boiled) | 4oz | 100gm | 230 |

| Food | Weight (average helping) | | Calories |
|------|--------|--------|---------:|
| salmon (smoked) | 2oz | 50gm | 95 |
| salmon (tinned)) | 3oz | 75gm | 120 |
| sardines (tinned) | 2oz | 50gm | 165 |
| sauerkraut | 4oz | 100gm | 25 |
| sausage (beef, cooked) | 4oz | 100gm | 325 |
| sausage (pork, cooked) | 4oz | 100gm | 325 |
| sausage (salami) | 2oz | 50gm | 185 |
| scallops (steamed) | 2oz | 50gm | 60 |
| scone | 1 scone | | 150 |
| semolina (dry) | 1oz | 25gm | 100 |
| semolina pudding | 4oz | 100gm | 160 |
| shepherds pie | 4oz | 100gm | 200 |
| shrimps (boiled) | 2oz | 50gm | 65 |
| skate (fried) | 4oz | 100gm | 210 |
| sole (fried) | 6oz | 150gm | 465 |
| sole (steamed) | 6oz | 150gm | 130 |
| soup (broth) | 8oz | 200gm | 145 |
| soup (consomme) | 8oz | 200gm | 40 |
| soup (cream) | 8oz | 200gm | 160 |
| soya flour | 1oz | 25gm | 120 |
| spaghetti (cooked) | 4oz | 100gm | 130 |
| steak (beef, grilled) | 4oz | 100gm | 345 |
| steak and kidney pie | 4oz | 100gm | 400 |
| strawberries (fresh) | 3oz | 75gm | 21 |
| strawberries (tinned) | 3oz | 75gm | 60 |
| sugar (brown) | 1oz | 25gm | 100 |
| sugar (white) | 1oz | 25gm | 100 |
| sultanas | 1oz | 25gm | 70 |
| swedes (turnips) | 2oz | 50gm | 15 |
| sweetbreads (fried) | 2oz | 50gm | 125 |
| sweetcorn | 3oz | 75gm | 80 |
| syrup | 1oz | 25gm | 85 |
| sweets (boiled) | 2oz | 50gm | 185 |
| Tangerine | 3oz | 75gm | 30 |
| tangerines (tinned) | 3oz | 75gm | 60 |
| tapioca (dry) | 1oz | 25gm | 100 |
| tea with lemon | 1 cup | | 5 |

| Food | Weight (average helping) | | Calories |
|---|---|---|---|
| tea with milk | 1 cup | | 20 |
| tea with milk and sugar | 1 cup | | 55 |
| toad in the hole | 4oz | 100gm | 330 |
| toast | 1oz | 25gm | 70 |
| tomato (fresh) | 2oz | 50gm | 10 |
| tomato (tinned) | 2oz | 50gm | 10 |
| tomato (fried) | 2oz | 50gm | 40 |
| tomato sauce (ketchup) | 1oz | 25gm | 30 |
| tongue | 2oz | 50gm | 170 |
| tripe (stewed) | 6oz | 150gm | 180 |
| trout (steamed) | 6oz | 150gm | 240 |
| tuna fish (tinned) | 3oz | 75gm | 200 |
| turkey (roast) | 2oz | 50gm | 110 |
| Veal (roast) | 2oz | 50gm | 135 |
| veal (stewed) | 3oz | 75gm | 190 |
| veal and ham pie | 3oz | 75gm | 320 |
| venison (roast) | 3oz | 75gm | 170 |
| Walnuts | 1oz | 25gm | 155 |
| watercress | 1oz | 25gm | 5 |
| whiting (fried) | 6oz | 150gm | 320 |
| whiting (steamed) | 6oz | 150gm | 160 |
| Yoghurt (natural) | ¼ pint | | 75 |
| | | 250ml | 130 |
| yoghurt (with fruit) | ¼ pint | | 150 |
| | | 250ml | 260 |
| yorkshire pudding | 2oz | 50gm | 120 |

**Alcohol**

| | | |
|---|---|---|
| Beer | 1 pint | 250 |
| brandy | 1oz | 75 |
| champagne | 3oz | 60 |
| cider | ½ pint | 110 |
| lager | 1 bottle | 175 |
| port | 2oz | 85 |

| Food | Weight (average helping) | Calories |
|---|---|---|
| sherry (dry) | 2oz | 70 |
| spirits (whisky, gin etc) | 1oz | 65 |
| stout | ½ pint | 100 |
| wine (dry) | 4oz | 80 |
| wine (sweet) | 4oz | 100 |

*Record your weight loss*: Don't expect to lose too much weight too soon. A slow but steady loss is likely to be more permanent. Keep a record of your weight each week; do not be tempted to weigh yourself every day since daily variations may be discouraging.

*If you want to put on weight*: There are, of course, some people who want to put on weight rather than lose it. Being too skinny can be just as frustrating as being too fat. Indeed it can be even more worrying since while the overweight know what they need to do to lose weight the underweight may feel that there is nothing they can do to put on weight. The simplest solution, of course, is to stick to a diet made up of high calorie foods. If this does not work it is worth checking with your doctor to make sure that there is no hidden reason for your inability to put on weight.

**Eating to stay healthy**

To stay healthy you do not only need to eat the right amount of food – you need to eat the right foods. Make up your daily calorie quota from different types of foods. Don't follow fad diets for more than a day at a time. If you do your body may run short of vital substances.

In addition to protein, carbohydrate and fats, you need a regular supply of vitamins. Taking extra vitamins will not cure a cold or even ward one off but if your body is short of vitamins you will be more susceptible to colds and flu. Don't waste money buying pills and bottles of medicine. Simply make sure that you eat a piece of fruit at least once a day. An orange or an apple will be enough. Use lemon juice in cooking and do not overboil green vegetables. Include a glass of fresh orange juice, grapefruit juice or pineapple juice at breakfast time.

Don't cut down your food intake too much during the winter months if you're trying to lose weight. When your body is cold it uses up energy faster than when it is warm. The thyroid and adrenal glands increase the output of hormones and a special defence mechanism hidden within the body triggers off an automatic shivering reflex. This is done to keep the body's temperature at a steady 36.9°C (98.4°F). Even though the temperature outside the body may be below freezing the temperature of the body must be kept up. Let the body temperature fall too much and you will die. Your basic metabolic rate may increase by a third in cold weather. Going out on a crash diet during the winter months will probably put you in bed when you should be going out to a party.

If you always seems to suffer from colds and flu more than others around you give your body a chance to fight off bugs by eating a little more. Watch your weight and if you don't put on a great deal of excess weight keep the extra calories in your diet until the end of the winter. Breakfast is a much more important meal than most people think it is. People trying to lose weight often miss it out entirely. That means that their bodies are fighting the daily battle without any ammunition at all. Make time to get some food into you before you leave home. A Dutch breakfast is fine. Cheese, ham and a glass of orange juice will provide you with plenty of healthy foodstuffs. Eat less in the evening when you'll be using up less calories. If you eat when you're keeping busy the food will be used up and not stored. If you eat in the evening when you're not using up calories the excess calories will be stored.

Remember, you are what you eat. Do you want to be a Choco Bar?

## When you have to diet

Sometimes you have to eat carefully in order to avoid triggering some existing disorder. Patients with dyspepsia, recurrent indigestion (see p. 172), gastritis or ulcer trouble (see p. 196) need to eat slowly, regularly and in fairly small quantities. They should rest after eating, avoid cigarettes and alcohol, fried foods, spicy, rich foods and strong tea or coffee. Hot and very cold food should also be avoided. Incidentally patients with stomach troubles who get a lot of wind should try and avoid struggling to bring up air – they'll probably only swallow more.

Patients with colitis or the irritable colon syndrome should stick to a smooth, non-irritating diet, avoiding fibre, pips, seeds and skins. Fizzy drinks, fried or fatty foods, alcohol and highly seasoned foods should also be avoided.

Constipated patients should eat plenty of fresh fruit, green vegetables and salads and drink lots of fluids. They should avoid too much starchy, sweet food – particularly cakes and buns.

Patients with gall bladder disease should avoid fatty or fried foods and so should patients with liver trouble. Liverish patients should also avoid alcohol.

Patients with heart disease (see p. 161) should avoid fats (particularly animal fats) and, since all men in the western world are potential heart attack victims, butter and other high fat content substances should be banned from the kitchen altogether.

## Why you need to exercise

Most of us can obtain water merely by turning a tap and light is ours at the flick of a switch. Outside the home we travel on aeroplanes and buses and drive ourselves in motor cars. All these mechanical aids reduce the amount of exercise we get. The office worker can often travel from home to office without more than a few dozen strides. He travels sitting down except when using the lift, complains if the car park is closed and he has to leave the car half a mile away, grumbles if the escalator isn't working and moans if he has to walk out to the aeroplane because there is no airport bus. Even schoolchildren have grown accustomed to the help of mechanical aids. They ride bicycles to school or travel by car. They use calculators to save them mental effort and television saves them the bother of actually standing in the cold to enjoy sports matches. If you think carefully you will probably find that every member of your family relies heavily upon gadgets and aids to help him through his day.

All this means that few of us get anywhere near enough exercise. And people who do not exercise are allowing their bodies to become incapable of coping with any extra strain or effort. The man who does no exercise will have atrophied muscles and a heart which can supply him with oxygen only so long as he continues to enjoy an undemanding existence.

When the sedentary husband runs for a bus or struggles to throw off a winter cold he will be using inadequate equipment. His heart may be able to manage as long as he continues to take things easy but when there is the slightest crisis his heart and his other organs will be less able to cope. Some people welcome motorized golf trolleys which enable golfers to play their sport without having to walk anywhere, remote control television buttons which save us the trouble of getting up to switch television channels and power driven tools which help us look after the garden without doing any manual work. But all this laziness has its price.

The man who takes no exercise and puts no demand on his body will have a weak heart, poor circulation and atrophied muscles. He will be in poor condition to withstand any physical or mental distress.

During the American Skylab experiments doctors found that astronauts who did no exercise while in space were weak and debilitated when they came back to earth whereas astronauts who did exercise came back relatively fit and healthy. What is true of the American astronauts is also true of your family. They may not be planning excursions to the moon but if you allow them to continue avoiding physical effort at every opportunity they will gradually become weaker and weaker. The human body is unlike any machine made by man. It actually thrives on hard work and becomes stronger the more it is used. Muscles, heart, lungs and so on all become more capable of coping with problems when they have all been well employed.

Professor Morris and colleagues at the London School of Hygiene and Tropical Medicine recently published a report in the *Lancet* which showed just how valuable exercise can be in helping to ward off heart trouble. The professor and his team questioned 16,882 British civil servants aged between forty and sixty-four and assessed their exercise habits. They then waited for the civil servants to have heart attacks. They discovered that while only 11 per cent of the civil servants who had been in the habit of taking regular exercise had heart disease no less than 26 per cent of those who did not take exercise succumbed to heart attacks. The team from London suggested that swimming, tennis, hill climbing, dancing, digging, running and tree felling were particularly effective forms of exercise.

Short periods of exercise done regularly improve the function of the heart and circulation as well as of the muscles, the cells of which increase in size and power after prolonged exercise. The muscles also develop more blood vessels. As a result of these improvements stamina increases and there is a greater tolerance to exercise. A dash for the bus or a climb upstairs when the lift is out of order becomes less of an ordeal. Exercise improves your general health. People who are fit fall ill less frequently, get better quicker when they are ill, feel and look brighter, are better able to cope with mental problems of all kinds and are less worried by anxiety and aggression.

### How fit are you?
Most people think they are fairly fit. A little overweight and out of condition perhaps but basically fit enough. You might admit that you ought to take more exercise and that extra exercise would make you feel better and brighter but you probably qualify this admission with a certain amount of unjustified confidence about your own physical condition.

It is easy to be quietly confident about your physical condition since you probably need to exert yourself only rarely. Most of us have no idea about our ability to run or jump simply because we do not commonly do either.

This section of the book is designed to help readers assess their own fitness and decide for themselves on fairly objective grounds whether or not they need to spend time on exercise. It is important to remember that these tests should not be tried by people recovering from any sort of physical problem, by people who develop pains or become breathless on doing ordinary household chores or by people taking prescribed pills. Anyone who does try the tests should stop if he or she develops unusual pains.

One of the simplest ways to assess your own body is to measure the ability of the heart to cope with extra stresses and strains. To do this you need nothing more sophisticated than an ordinary step and a watch. The step should be about twelve inches deep and the watch should be calibrated in seconds. If you cannot find a step with a twelve inch drop, a low bench or stool should be suitable.

For three minutes simply step up twenty four times a minute. In three minutes you will have climbed a total of 72 steps.

Each step consists of four movements. Step up with your right foot and then move your left foot up alongside your right foot. Next step down with the right foot and then step down with the left foot.

When you have completed the exercise sit down and after waiting for five seconds, measure your heart rate during the following minute. The pulse rate after the exercise will give you some idea of your general fitness. If your pulse rate is below 80 per minute then you are very fit. If it is between 80 and 100 then you are of average fitness. If it is over 100 then you are unfit. If the pulse rate is over 130 you are really in bad shape.

There are several other tests which can be done by ordinary people in their own homes without expensive equipment. Persuade a friend to hold on to your ankles while you lie on your back on the floor. Then clasp your hands behind your head and try to sit up, keeping your knees bent so that your thigh and lower leg form an angle of ninety degrees.

Now touch your right knee with your left elbow. Lie down, pull yourself up and continue with the exercise then touch your left knee with your right elbow. Count the number of times you make contact in one minute. The average man will manage 20 to 30 of these movements in a minute. A fit man will do more and an unfit man will do less. The average woman will manage a similar number but the total range will be greater. A very fit woman will probably manage 50 while an unfit woman will only manage 2 or 3.

An even simpler way to measure your fitness is to measure the amount of time you take to cover a fixed distance either running or walking. Every man and woman should be able to cover a mile in 12 minutes under their own steam. Anyone who cannot is not fit.

All these tests are described in more detail in the *Official Y.M.C.A. Physical Fitness Handbook* by Clayton R. Myers.

**What sort of exercise should you do?**

It is important to do the right kind of exercise and to do the right amount of it. To be fit you do not have to be able to lift a mini car with one hand or bend a poker into a horseshoe with one swift movement.

When you take up exercise do it slowly. Unexpected and unusual amounts of exercise can prove fatal. The man who has had a heart attack and who joins a local athletic club or basketball team is likely to find himself back in bed in the local coronary care unit before the end of the first event he appears in. It is important that all convalescent competitors begin gingerly and stop whatever they are doing as soon as any pain, particularly chest pain, appears. Of 21 deaths which occurred among sportsmen and were reported in a paper published in the *Lancet* in 1975, 18 were thought to have been due to heart attacks occurring during or shortly after sport. Some of these sportsmen had undoubtedly made the mistake of taking up exercise too quickly. They would have been wiser to start slowly.

The simplest type of exercise is walking. The patient with a heart condition should begin to take exercise within a few weeks of leaving his sick bed. The easiest way to see just how far he can walk is for him to walk until he begins to suffer slight pain and then to stop. The first signs of anginal pain are a warning that it is time to take a break. He could carry a book with him to help pass a few minutes while he rests. A mere twenty minutes walking a day can have a dramatic effect on the condition of the heart.

The best sports for the exercising man who wants to improve his health and prepare himself for the strains of day to day life are sports which are not competitive. Americans surveys have shown that runners live on average fourteen years longer than football players. The team player has an obligation to his fellow players as well as to team followers. The individual has an obligation only to himself. He can take it easy and enjoy his sport. A Finnish study published in 1974 showed the benefit of ski-ing, an essentially lonely sport in which the competitor fights against the clock rather than against a visible opponent. The induced distress is minimal. Winning or losing, getting selection, keeping a place and fitting in with organized training schedules are all additions to the strain of modern living.

Keep fit classes, health and beauty courses and physical culture groups are easy to find. There are dozens of good books explaining the values of isometric exercises and courses are available showing how to build muscles with the aid of weight-lifting equipment. Despite the fact that many of us pay large sums of money to relieve us of physical exertion there are many companies engaged in selling equipment designed to help us keep fit by exercising. Some of the equipment sold is very simple. There are, for example, wooden or metal bars available which can be fitted into door frames and used either for simply hanging on to or for practising chin-ups. Other far more expensive items are also available. There are bicycles which will never get anywhere and rowing machines which will never get wet. There are even jogging machines which enable you to jog endlessly on multiple small nylon rollers fitted onto a slightly inclined frame.

There is, however, nothing a machine can help you do that you cannot do yourself without a machine. Exercises which involve movement are best; you are more likely to help keep your weight down and the exercise is likely to be more interesting. Walking, jogging, running, swimming, cycling, hill climbing, tennis and squash are good dynamic exercises. Swimming is good because it uses most of the muscles of the body. Jogging, which has become very fashionable, simply means running slowly. People who are in poor condition, overweight or more than forty-five years old should begin by walking before they run.

A number of problems peculiar to joggers have been described in the medical literature. Researchers have shown, for example, that 31 per cent of female athletes report breast problems. Many complain of abrasions caused by slipping bra straps. Dr Christine Maycock, the Associate Professor of Surgery at New Jersey Medical School has attached tracers to the wobbling nipples of joggers and drawn graphs which have helped her to design suitable underwear. Maternity bras seem most effective. Dr Fred Levitt of North Western University Medical School has suggested that joggers who do not wear bras and who develop sore nipples can protect themselves with vaseline or some other similar product. Male joggers in New England have reported penile frost bite. No researchers have yet designed special underwear to protect against this eventuality but they no doubt will in due course.

Whatever the exercise chosen the general rule for beginners is: if it hurts, stop.

### Why do people smoke?

Many smokers claim that tobacco helps them cope with difficult situations, manage their relationships with other people more effectively and stops them losing their temper when aggrieved. Psychologists suggest that smokers are usually searching for love, attention and support and that the appearance of independence and virility common among smokers is a false one: they are in reality sensitive people with only a veneer of sophistication and worldliness.

It certainly seems true that many smokers use cigarettes as a spiritual crutch, taking up the weed again at times of crisis and lighting up most frequently when angry, worried or depressed. Many smokers simply find themselves lighting up out of habit. Without really being aware of it they find themselves reaching for cigarettes and matches and without there being any conscious action involved they have cigarettes in their mouths. This habit may recur during times of boredom or nervousness as well as in times of trouble.

However, although smoking helps people deal with difficult moments and remain calm when they might otherwise panic it does only provide a temporary and short-lived symptomatic solution.

## The hazards of smoking

At the beginning of 1978 Joseph Califano, America's Secretary of Health, Education and Welfare described smoking as a form of slow motion suicide and assessed it as America's Public Enemy Number 1. He said that smoking was a major factor in 220,000 deaths a year from heart disease in America and 100,000 cancer related deaths. He reckoned the annual cost to America as £10,000 million. The Royal College of Surgeons in Britain have estimated that habitual smokers who go through 20 cigarettes a day lose a minute of their lives for every minute they spend smoking. Put bluntly that means that a smoker who goes through a pack of 20 each day will live five years less than someone who doesn't smoke at all. Something like 40 per cent of all smokers can expect to die as a direct result of their addiction.

The relationship of smoking to lung cancer, bronchitis and other types of chest infection is well known. Less well publicized however, is the relationship of smoking to heart disease. It is known now that cigarette smoking actually decreases the efficiency of the heart. Below the age of forty-five smokers are fifteen times more likely to have heart disease than are non-smokers. Cigarettes also have a bad effect on the stomach, both helping to produce ulcers and preventing the healing of existing ulcers. Arteries in the limbs are also often damaged.

Many smokers dismiss the dangers of smoking by arguing that they have known heavy smokers who have been unaffected by tobacco. One man I met, for example, insisted that his father had smoked fifty cigarettes a day for half a century without having any physical illness at all. That is rather like arguing that because some people have survived serious car crashes without injury there is no need to avoid serious car crashes. For every smoker you can produce who claims that smoking never harmed him I can produce ten who will agree that smoking did damage their health.

You will undoubtedly read reports from time to time which dismiss the evidence which convicts the cigarette as a killer. Those reports are usually produced by commercial organizations with a very expensive axe to grind. The fact that doctors

87

as a professional group smoke far fewer cigarettes than they smoked a decade ago is good evidence to suggest that the medical proof to convict tobacco of causing physical damage is convincing. If you stop smoking your health will not only stop deteriorating, it will very probably improve. Cigarette smokers who give up the habit are usually astonished to see the rubbish they cough up in the weeks following giving up cigarettes. Heart, lungs and stomach will all work more effectively when cigarettes have been abandoned. And as I have already pointed out, a fit person is far better able to cope with physical and mental pressures. Give up cigarettes and in due course you will not need them. You will be better able to cope.

### Giving it up!
Any method of giving up smoking that works is a good one. Some people claim that they have helped kick the habit by taking tablets bought from the chemist that give cigarettes a nasty taste, by chewing gum or eating peppermints or by going to a hypnotist and being told to give up smoking while in a trance. One man gave up smoking and took to eating prunes. Soon he was a twenty prune a day man. I don't know what effect the change in diet had on his bowel habit but I imagine he might have been kept too busy to bother about lighting up a cigarette.

Smokers with an economical mind find that it helps to write down each day just how much money they have saved by not smoking. It is astonishing to see just how much money is saved in one week. By the end of a month it is frightening for a moderately heavy smoker to see what would have literally gone up in smoke.

One method is to change the brand of cigarette you smoke every day. This makes life difficult because you have to keep looking for new brands and it makes smoking less pleasant. Some cigarettes will be stronger and some will be weaker than those usually enjoyed. Buy cigarettes from a different shop, never buy more than one pack at once, buy in packs of ten and try to remember to forget to take a pack with you when you go out.

It often helps to make up rules to govern your smoking habit. This helps because it eases you out of the habit a little at a time. To begin with, cut out smoking during working hours; then stop smoking at meal times; do not smoke while watching television. After a few days make sure that you don't smoke when doing anything else at all. Give up smoking in the car or on the bus. On a train or aeroplane book a seat in a non-smoking compartment. Cut out smoking room by room. On one day swear to yourself that you'll never smoke in the bedroom again. On the next day give up smoking in the bathroom. Go through your home room by room and soon you'll be reduced to standing on the doorstep smoking a furtive cigarette. At that point giving up is a relief.

### A salutary illustration

The permanent contribution that changes in diet, exercise and cigarette consumption can make to the physical and mental well-being of the ordinary man was vividly illustrated by the extraordinary discovery that American navy pilots and navigators who were taken prisoner by the North Vietnamese were healthier when examined after their release than a similar group of fliers who had not been captured. The prisoners had been kept physically fit, deprived of alcohol, excessive fats and tobacco and stress-producing paperwork. Their peers, who had been allowed access to all the usually accepted privileges of a Western society suffered far more from physical and mental illness.

## LEARNING TO RELAX

There are numerous organizations, some of them quasi-religious, a few of them founded by genuinely well-meaning people but most of them run by unashamedly commercial enterprises, which offer courses, equipment and expensive advice to people anxious to learn how to relax and how to cope with their own susceptibility to outside disorders and personal distresses. Many of these organizations offer their own special variation on the theme of relaxation but often there is an accompanying requirement for some more general commitment. This need for commitment frightens off many who would otherwise be interested in learning how to relax but who find the prospect of adopting a distinctive and unusual life style rather frightening. The shaven, saffron-robed and chanting drop-outs so familiar in most of the world's major cities have given all forms of meditation and relaxation a bad name and frightened off many millions who might otherwise have benefited from the physical and mental advantages of meditation. The unusual and, for many, difficult physical positions adopted by the exponents of yoga have made that discipline too eccentric for many more. Biofeedback machinery is difficult to obtain and expensive and there are therefore very few readers of this book who are likely to be able to take advantage of any of the benefits offered by this new technique.

The truth is that to benefit from relaxation you do not have to join an organization, buy any equipment or attend any courses. If you want to avoid stress diseases you can. That is the only requirement – motivation; with it you will succeed, without it you will fail.

For most of us, changing our environment by dropping out of work and leaving home to enjoy the comforts of a begging bowl-maintained commune is not possible. Responsibilities, ambitions and pride make such wholesale abdication of social duties impractical. The alternative is to adapt our own responses to the existing environment. And that is both possible and practical. It is perfectly possible for anyone, clerk, labourer, executive, housewife, student or highly paid professional to learn to discriminate between realistic and unrealistic fears and anxieties and to learn when aggressive reactions are appropriate or inappropriate. By learning and acknowledging which situations are likely to produce distress we can all learn to anticipate trouble and therefore to annul much of its effect on our bodies. It is the unexpectedness and inexplicability of most crises which cause most anguish. In addition we can all learn the simple secrets of how to relax properly and to gain the physical and mental advantages which relaxation offers.

## The scientific background

Using relaxation to help cure and prevent genuine physical illnesses is not new. It has been known for years that rest is an
excellent remedy for peptic ulceration, high blood pressure,
pulmonary tuberculosis, heart trouble and many infective diseases. Relaxation was recommended for patients with high
blood pressure in a book entitled, *Progressive Relaxation, a
physiological and clinical investigation of muscular states and
their significance in psychology and medical practice*, published
in 1929 and written by Dr Edmund Jacobson.

Dr Jacobson recognized that not everyone finds relaxing easy.
He pointed out that it is helpful to learn to recognize the signs
of residual tension and listed irregular fast breathing movements, wrinkling of the forehead and voluntary movements of
the limbs. The fully relaxed person has a clear mind and slow
regular breathing; occasionally there will be involuntary
twitches of muscles as tension drains away but there will be no
voluntary muscular movements.

Learning to relax is rather like learning to do anything else
– you need practice in the beginning. You wouldn't expect to be
able to dance the watz or play a round of golf without some
practice. Relaxing is easier but it still needs a little preparation.
As you get better at it so the relaxing will be more effective and
as you go through the necessary actions automatically so you
will get better at relaxing, just as when you learn to dance without thinking of where your feet are all the time you will dance
more smoothly.

In *Scientific American* in 1972 two American researchers,
one an Assistant Professor of Medicine at Harvard Medical
School, published results which showed that during meditation
oxygen consumption and metabolic rates markedly decreased
(more than in sleep or hypnosis) and that it is possible to
measure a reduction in the level of anxiety recorded by people
meditating. Physiologists in France and America have shown
that some meditators can learn to slow or stop their hearts and
in 1970 a writer in the *Lancet* showed evidence that breathing
rates per minute drop significantly during meditation. German
researchers at the University of Cologne have shown that medi-

tators have reduced levels of aggression, depression, irritability and nervousness and researchers at Stanford Research Institute have shown that those who learn meditation manage without, or with smaller doses of, psychotropic drugs such as Valium and Librium.

In an article published in the *Lancet* in July 1975 a London general practitioner reported on work which she had done with some hypertensive patients. The patients were divided into two groups: one group went along to the surgery regularly for three months and spent half an hour relaxing on a couch, the other group spent the same amount of time at the surgery and received the same amount of attention but were taught how to relax properly and how to meditate. While the patients in the first group did show some fall in blood pressure patients in the second group showed a spectacular improvement and nine months later the improvement still persisted.

Despite the fact that this technique costs very little to teach and nothing to practise, is perfectly safe and free of side effects and can obviate the need for hypertensive drugs there have been few other British attempts to produce similar results. The reason may perhaps be that much medical research is done by or sponsored on behalf of commercial companies and no commercial company manufacturing drugs is going to be very interested in a technique which does not involve the consumption of a marketable product. Neither drug manufacturers nor doctors have much interest in promoting a treatment method which needs neither of them. Even patients have been persuaded to be suspicious of treatments which do not entail regular pill popping.

### The physical approach to relaxation
To relax your body you must learn just how your muscles feel when they are tight and tense. Clench your fist and you'll feel the muscles of your hand and forearm tight and firm. Now let your fist unfold and you'll feel the muscles relax. To relax properly all you have to do is stiffen and then relax the muscles of your body group by group.

When you first start learning to relax you should choose a

quiet, private place where you are not likely to be interrupted and where stimuli are least disturbing. It's difficult to begin relaxing in a busy, crowded office or bus although you will be able to do just that eventually. Lie down in a darkened room where you are alone and unlikely to be disturbed. Allow a quarter of an hour and plan to spend that much time each day for a week until you have mastered the art of physical relaxation. (You will not have to relax step by step as you become more experienced – you will learn how to relax your entire body more or less instantly). You will begin to feel better after just one session. You will feel calmer and more relaxed and your body will feel fresher and your mind will be more alert.

**The twenty steps to a relaxed body;**
1 Clench your left hand as tightly as you can, making a fist with the fingers. Do it well and you will see the knuckles go white. If you now let your fist unfold you will feel the muscles relax. When your hand was clenched the muscles were tensed; unfolded the same muscles are relaxed. This is what you must do with the other muscle groups of your body. '

2 Bend your left arm and try to make your left biceps muscle stand out as much as you can. Then relax and let the muscles ease. Let your arm lie loosely by your side and ignore it.

3 Relax your right hand in the same way.

4 Relax your right biceps muscle in the same way.

5 Tighten the muscles in your left foot. Curl your toes. When the foot feels as tense as you can make it let it relax.

6 Tense the muscles of your left calf. If you reach down you can feel the muscles at the back of your leg firm up as you tense them. Bend your foot back at the ankle to help tighten up the muscles. Then let the muscles relax.

7 Straighten your leg and push your foot away from you. You will feel the muscles on the front of your thigh tighten up; they should be firm right up to the top of your leg.

8 Relax your right foot.

9 Relax your right lower leg.

10 Relax your right thigh.

11 Lift yourself up by tightening up your buttock muscles. You will be able to lift your body upwards by an inch or so. Then let the muscles fall loose again.

12 Tense and contract your abdominal muscles. Try to pull your abdominal wall as far in as possible. Then let go and allow your waist to reach its maximum circumference.

13 Tighten the muscles of your chest. Take a big deep breath in and strain to hold it for as long as possible. Then let go.

14 Push your shoulders backwards as far as they will go, then turn them forwards and inwards. Finally shrug them as high as you can. Keep your head perfectly stil and try to touch your ears with your shoulders. It will probably be impossible but try anyway. Then let your shoulders relax and ease.

15 Next tighten up the muscles of your back. Try to make yourself as tall as you can. Then let the muscles relax.

16 The muscles of the neck are next. Lift your head forwards and pull at the muscles at the back of your neck. Turn your head first one way and then the other. Push your head backwards with as much force as you can. Then let the muscles of your neck relax. Move it about to make sure that it really is completely loose and easy.

17 Move your eyebrows upwards and then pull them down as far as they will go. Do this several times making sure that you can feel the muscles tightening both when you move the eyebrows up and when you can pull them down. Then let them relax.

18 Screw up your eyes as tightly as you can. Pretend that someone is trying to force your eyes open. Keep them shut tightly. Then, keeping your eyelids closed let them relax.

19 Move your lower jaw around. Grit your teeth. Wrinkle your nose. Smile as wide as you can showing as many teeth as you have got. Now let all these facial muscles relax.

20 Push your tongue out as far as it will go, push it firmly against the bottom of your mouth and the top of your mouth and then let it lie relaxed and easy inside your mouth.

Remember as you do these simple exercises that your breathing should be slow, deep and regular. Take deep breaths and breathe as slowly as you comfortably can.

## The mental approach to relaxation

Teachers of transcendental meditation suggest that their students adopt a mantra, or secret word or phrase (usually meaningless) which is repeated over and over again to help exclude all extraneous thoughts from the mind. The best known mantra is hari krishna, but most followers of the Maharishi Yogi have their own personal mantra which acts for them as a code word, enabling them to relax easily and speedily. Objects will do just as well as words and you can, if you wish, choose an object to keep in your mind's eye as you drift into a calmer state. Choose something which doesn't stimulate you or else your attempts to drift off will prove unsuccessful. The young man who concentrates on the imaginary unclothed form of the nearest woman will remain quite tense and anxious.

If emptying your mind is too difficult and you simply can't clear away all the thoughts and anxieties which are there then try to replace them with a calmer, more relaxing scene. Establishing a void can be difficult whereas establishing a well-remembered peaceful scene is much easier. Remember a pleasant peaceful day on the beach or in the country. Imagine you are sitting there with only the sound of the sea or the feel of the sun on your face to stimulate your senses. As you drift off check to make sure that your brow is not furrowed and your eyes not screwed up. Keep your face free of tensions as you think about your peaceful scene. Slowly, as you relax more and more you'll find your mind emptying of everything, even the scene you've conjured up. Your day-dream will have led you gently into full and effective relaxation.

Feel your own pulse (use the forefinger of your left hand which you should press lightly against the radial artery which can be found in the area of the base of your right thumb) and count the number of beats in a minute. If you measure your pulse rate when you are physically or mentally excited you will find that your heart has quickened. Run up a flight of stairs and you will find that your heart rate has probably exceeded a hundred beats per minute. If you are worrying about the boss's reaction to the fact that you have just lost £5 million worth of orders then your pulse rate will also rise. You will feel your pulse rate drop when you have exchanged the troublesome thoughts in your mind by more peaceful memories.

**Using the techniques of relaxation**
Next time you are in a traffic jam take a look around you at the other motorists. There will be one fellow hunched over the steering wheel, white knuckles tightly clenched. Another will be scowling and frowning as he taps the steering wheel impatiently with his fingers. A third will be gritting his teeth, studying his wrist watch at thirty second intervals and banging his horn imperiously. All those drivers are using many muscles they do not need and are wasting energy and effort; they will finish their journeys with headaches, neckaches and backaches.

It is not only motorists who use muscles unnecessarily when tensed. Office workers, hunched over paperwork with eyes screwed up and schoolchildren huddled over homework are equally likely to suffer from muscle fatigue. Apart from causing simple headaches and muscular pains in the neck, back and limbs, muscle contractions and tensing can also make high blood pressure higher by squeezing on blood vessels and sending blood around the body at a much faster rate than normal. It is not the anxiety or the patient's mental response to his problems which causes the high blood pressure but his physical response. By learning to relax and ease his tightened muscles the patient can bring his blood pressure down. He doesn't have to actually solve his problem and he doesn't have to try to 'just forget'.

Get into the habit of checking on yourself to see if you are unnecessarily tensing muscles. Look in the mirror if there is one handy, if there isn't then simply try and look at yourself as others might. Are your eyes screwed up? Are your eyebrows pulled down? Is your jaw set tight? Are you clenching your teeth? There are dozen of muscles involved in these simple movements and unnecessary use of these muscles can cause infuriating aches and pains. Go through the rest of your body.

Are your fingers tapping unnecessarily? Are your fists clenched? Are your legs held tightly under your chair? Get into the
habit of relaxing your muscles wherever you are.

The theorists say that to relax you should lie down and allow
your limbs to drift weightlessly. That's a fine theory but in practice the boss isn't likely to look upon you kindly if you suddenly
lie down on the office floor. He may get the wrong idea. School
teachers won't be overcome with kindly emotions if their
charges insist on bringing pillows and cushions into the classroom, and shop assistants won't be greatly pleased if half way
through the afternoon, in the middle of the sales, half their
customers down bags and relax on the nearest piece of comfortable furniture. You must therefore develop the knack of
relaxing your muscles wherever you may be. Take a minute off
from whatever it is you are doing and allow your muscles to
relax. Go through systematically from limb to limb and you'll
be better able to deal with your traffic jam, office work or shopping without acquiring a splitting headache and without developing high blood pressure. Control your breathing since this is
one of the easiest ways to control your heart rate and your
body's other reactions to distress.

If it is possible, find somewhere to sit down. Shutting your
eyes may help by cutting out the visual stimuli that so often
prove irresistible distractions. If you cannot shut your eyes then
keep your eyes fixed on some inanimate object such as a lamp
post or a chair and let them stay there. If you have been practising properly and learned how to relax then you will benefit a
great deal. The crowds will still be there, the paperwork will
still be piled high and the problems won't have gone away but
you will be much better able to cope.

## Living the peaceful life
If two people are given identical tasks to complete they will
inevitably react in different ways. One will calmly and systematically identify what must be done while the other may panic
right from the beginning. While the first person is deciding how
best to approach his task the second might be rushing about
aimlessly, using up a great deal of energy, becoming physically
and mentally exhausted but getting nothing done.

The second person, who as well as working in haste, very probably moves and speaks quickly, puts himself or herself under tremendous pressure and builds up a great deal of physical and mental tension. The more thoughtful character, who approaches life more calmly, will be able to withstand more pressure and more problems before becoming tense.

It is not easy, of course, to change your basic approach to life – but it is possible. Try to think carefully and as objectively as possible about how you react under pressure. If you are a bustler and you rush about getting very little done you will know it. If you tend to talk too much and say too little I doubt if you will need anyone else to tell you about it.

You won't be able to change the way you work overnight but once you have made the decision to try you will be able to make slow but certain progress. You should find that you will be able to do just as much but at a far lower cost to your own health.

**The advantages of organization**

If a builder tried to erect a cathedral without any architectural plans he would probably be lamentably unsuccessful. On a less spectacular scale the same is true for those of us trying to cope with relatively simple and more mundane problems. Planning can often reduce stresses and prevent problems arising. The housewife who makes a shopping list and ensures that she buys everything she needs on a single visit to the supermarket will have fewer domestic problems to sort out than the housewife who makes no list but buys on impulse. The motorist who remembers to have his car serviced and to keep the gas tank filled will have fewer unexpected breakdown than the motorist who is quite disorganized. The student who decides at the beginning of each academic year just how much work has to be done and how long can be allocated to each project will have a much better chance of completing his syllabus than the student who makes no plans but insists on struggling through his course on a day to day basis. The secretary who orders stationery in advance, before she runs out, will have far fewer crises than the secretary who never keeps stocks of paper or pencils and who always has to beg or borrow stocks at inconvenient times.

To organize your life effectively, efficiently and painlessly:

1 Keep a notebook and pencil in your pocket or handbag at all times. Jot down points you want to remember wherever you are. That way you wil no longer have to spend hours wondering what it was you were so anxious to get done or puzzling over that knot in your handkerchief. Notebooks are better than diaries because you aren't limited in space. A diary large enough to provide you with note making space to last a year would be too big to carry around.

2 Keep a diary as well and get into the habit of examining it each morning to make sure you haven't forgotten any appointments or arrangements. Put a note in your diary about a week ahead of all birthdays and anniversaries. That way you should have time to make purchases without too much haste.

3 Keep a filing system at home to enable you to keep bills, receipts and important letters neatly and safely. If, like many people, you just stuff bills and letters into odd drawers you'll waste hours when you need information or proof of purchase. Clear out your files once a year and relegate out dated paperwork to the loft, or the garbage can. If you don't want to buy a proper metal filing cabinet use old brown envelopes – as big as you can get them. Simply write a brief description of the contents on the outside of each envelope and then keep all envelopes in one drawer.

4 When you're planning some special event (such as a large party or celebration or a move) keep a special master plan to help you keep things running smoothly. List everything that has to be done and then mark off the dates by which time each problem must be solved. If you're planning a party, for example, you may need to organize caterers, liquor supplies, food purchases, printing of invitations, distribution of invitations, entertainment, parking facilities and many other things according to the style of the party. If the printer forgets to produce your invitations and you forget to remind him your party may be light on guests.

### Survival in a changing society
The time between having an idea and applying it generally has

shrunk to a fraction of what it used to be. The typewriter was first patented in 1714 but was not widely available until the middle of the twentieth century. Inventions patented this year will be on general sales next year at the very latest. By the time a child of today grows up the information he was taught at school will probably be out of date. Scientists are accumulating information at such an alarming rate that not even specialists can keep up with the advances in their own field. The industrial revolution has been taken over by an administrative revolution. More than half of all the people employed in the Western world are involved in service industries. Progress in all spheres of human endeavour is increasing much faster now than at any time in the past.

In the United States of America, the United Kingdom, Northern Italy, Germany and Sweden where life has always been relatively fast it has become unbearably fast for many people. In Spain, Mexico, Arabia and Southern Italy where life has until recently been taken at a more leisurely pace the acceleration is now becoming noticeable. The acquisitive and throwaway society is spreading. Disposable razors, tooth-brushes, cigarette lighters and torches are available internationally. (In the United Kingdom things have begun to turn full circle. I recently saw an advertisement promoting the virtues of a non-disposable dust bag for a vacuum cleaner.) The increase in the number of disposables available merely highlights the lack of durability and certainty in our modern world.

Transience, novelty and diversity are as Alvin Toffler points out so vividly in his book *Future Shock* a part of modern life. Buildings are knocked down within a decade of their being erected. In big cities there is an almost permanent sequence of evacuations, demolitions, rebuildings, furnishings, inhabitings and evacuations. Clothes are expected to last only a season. Children exchange their toys annually. Even small girls part with their old dolls happily as new models appear first in the shops and then underneath the Christmas tree. Television personalities often have careers lasting in terms of months rather than years. Children's crazes for such items as hoola hoops and skateboards come and go annually. Motorists decorate their vehicles with sticky labels one year and personalized sun shields the next. Today's settlers travel more during their lifetimes than did yesterday's nomads. In 1914 the typical American travelled about, 1,500 miles a year. Today there must be few who do not travel ten times that amount and think nothing of it. By the time a telephone book is printed it will be out of date. Job turnover in many countries is running at 30 to 40 per cent each year.

The bureaucrats of today have extraordinary powers. The American Commission on Federal Paperwork created in 1974 estimates that the US government produces enough documents every year to fill 51 major league baseball stadiums. One American company, E. I. Du Pont de Nemours and Co estimated that they have to spend 5 million dollars annually producing some 15,000 reports for government departments. When the Lockheed Aircraft Corporation planned to build new air transport planes they needed an 11,000 man organization to control the administration of the venture. In the British National Health Service there are more administrators than doctors and nurses. Gerald Ford estimated that American bureaucracy costs the typical American family 2,000 dollars a year.

Different bureaucratic departments often make different demands. The American organization, Occupational Safety and Health Administration demands grated floors in butchers shops to stop employees slipping over. The Department of Agriculture, however, insists that floors must be smooth to reduce the risk of infection. The OSHA insists that sausage-making machines have protective guards whereas the Department of Agriculture has regulations which say that such guards are not to be used since they make the machines too difficult to clean.

These problems are increasing rather than reducing. And because communications systems are also improving and providing us with more tightly written, information-packed messages we are made more aware of the regulations and the penalties for ignoring them.

Alvin Toffler describes 'future shock' as the 'dizzying disorientation brought on by the premature arrival of the future'. Certainly many people do find themselves in an almost permanent state of 'shock' as a result of the changes which occur daily in our societies. The solutions many people choose to help them cope often merely add to the problems facing their neighbours. For example, society is currently breaking into small groups of people with associated industrial skills who try to declare and register their independence by using their skills to enable them to negotiate higher pay settlements. Inevitably, this breakdown of society means that everyone suffers for the more complex a society the easier it is to disrupt. The truth is that today in our highly developed societies we are all dependent on one another. The coal miner needs the power worker who needs the train driver who needs the fireman who needs the refuse collector who needs the hospital orderly.

It is, of course, practically impossible for any individual to halt progress. Changes will inevitably continue. One problem is that technological questions will be come more and more complex and lay authorities will be less and less likely to have the knowledge or understanding to enable them to discuss solutions critically and sensibly. Scientific research already needs monitoring and yet who but the scientist is fit to do the monitoring?

There are, however, ways in which you and I can have some control over our own destinies and reduce the common feeling of frustration and impotence.

*Firstly*, you can support organizations which stimulate and criticize official bodies. Consumer protection agencies, as long as they remain independent of governments and are allowed to develop sufficient strength can protect us all against commercial excesses.

*Secondly*, you can learn to regard bureaucratic institutions with scepticism and a healthy lack of respect. When a form arrives for you to fill in find out why the information is needed, if you have a legal obligation to provide the information and what channels there are enabling you to protest if you feel that the provision of the information would be an infringement of your personal freedom. If the law says that you have to fill a form in does it say that you have to tell the whole truth? Ambiguities are often present in official forms.

*Thirdly*, you can make it known that you are in favour of open government. Even though you may not understand the workings of the Central Genetic Control Committee it is in your interests for the minutes of the Committee meetings to be made available. Someone who *does* understand and who is suspicious will read them if they're available. Information kept secret is much more dangerous.

*Fourthly*, you can share your particular problems with others who have the same difficulties. Organizations formed by people protesting about the development of new roadways, the closure of railways and the building of industrial plants in residential areas have often been successful. Protesting undoubtedly eases frustration. Sufferers from specific disorders often gain strength as well as information from joining societies run by others with identical problems.

*Fifthly*, you can help your children learn how to adapt, how to assess new information and how to cope with change. Present educational methods are based on outdated needs. Today's facts are simply tomorrow's history. Today's children need to be taught how to value information and how to assess its worth critically and efficiently. Science fiction can help children come to terms more easily with the rapid changes likely in the future. Jules Verne, H. G. Wells, George Orwell and Aldous Huxley all forecast the future with uncanny skill. The best of today's science fiction writers have similar abilities.

*Sixthly*, you can learn to cope with minor problems at home more effectively. It is becoming more and more difficult to get hold of repairmen, doctors and handymen. The person who can deal with minor problems of illness and material fragility himself or herself will be less dependent and therefore more confident. The man who cannot do minor repairs to his house will suffer much more distress than the man who can. The woman who doesn't know what to do with her children when they have minor rashes and colds will be distressed and distraught if unable to obtain expert advice. It is, in addition, wise to provide yourself with alternative forms of cooking, lighting and heating so that emergencies produced by industrial action can be endured with minimum hardship. There will undoubtedly be a power cut sometime during the next year so stock up with candles now in preparation rather than waiting until the candle shops are crowded with panicking buyers.

Minor frustrations which we think we ought to be able to cope with but which prove insoluble produce a great deal of stress. In addition there is often the stress involved in trying to get hold of someone who does have the necessary skills and is prepared to make them available at a reasonable price.

## The escape clause

The simplest way for a man to avoid distress is for him to change his way of life. Some people simply opt out for short periods at a time. Charles Darwin used to become ill to give himself an excuse to rest in bed. So did Florence Nightingale, Marcel Proust, Sigmund Freud and many others.

Some take their breaks in longer chunks; disappearing to the seaside for a fortnight at a time once a year. Unhappily today many people spend their holiday period struggling to accumulate a new series of exotic experiences and photographs with which to entertain the neighbours at home. Such a holiday merely contributes to the holidaymakers' annual accumulation of distress rather than helping to in any way diminish it. A growing number are taking weekend breaks; buying mobile homes and touring wild countryside away from the mailman and the telephone or buying small dilapidated country cabins and living rough without mains sewage or colour television. The psychological value of having a retreat available is often enormous. Inevitably, of course, there are some who are determined to improve the market value of their temporary weekend domicile by introducing all the services they originally went there to escape!

In addition there are many people who are making the complete break and abandoning the fast city life for the quieter, healthier country existence. Of course, there are people for whom city life is a tonic but many of those who live the city life are *not* suited to it. Carthorses are not anatomically or physiologically capable of running as fast as racehorses. They are designed for different work. If forced into regular racing they will be generally unsuccessful and probably unhappy. Less ambitious activities are likely to prove more satisfying and relaxing.

According to a report in *Time* magazine (15 March, 1976) between 1970 and 1974 over 1.7 million more Americans left the big metropolitan areas than moved into them. New York alone lost half a million more people than it gained and Chicago's loss amounted to a quarter of a million people. Country areas gained inhabitants at a tremendous pace – Western Arizona, the slopes of the Rockies and parts of the Great Lakes all acquiring citizens. Some fled in search of 'nature' and a return to 'real living'; most, however, left for more practical reasons. They left in the hope that in the smaller cities and towns there would be greater scope for their skills. They left to escape the growing amount of crime in all the major cities, to avoid the overcrowding, pollution, noise and traffic queues, to escape the rapidly deteriorating quality of life and in the hope of finding a little civility and community spirit. One young female anaesthetist who left San Francisco for a much smaller town sixty miles away pointed out that before moving she had needed an escort when leaving the hospital for the parking lot at night. Others have talked of the depressive effects of living in a city where triple bolted doors are normal and where a cheerful greeting in the street arouses fear rather than friendship. Those who migrate also point out that with the aid of a motor car the big city attractions are rarely more than an hour or two away. It can often take just as long to commute to work from suburbia at peak time.

Whether you choose the weekend break, the annual holiday by the coast or in the country or an occasional day in bed make sure your escapes are genuine and helpful. Resist the temptation to allow your quiet times to acquire the distressing aspects of normal weekday life. If you can't stand the prospect of having no running water or flush toilets then do not buy or rent a country cabin without mains facilities. If you become itchy and uncomfortable after two days with nothing to do do not plan to spend a month on the beach. If you hate driving don't spend your summer break driving round Europe and struggling to keep to a busy schedule.

If you plan a more permanent break to free yourself of some of the more distressing aspects of big city life make sure that you aren't stepping out from the frying pan right into the fire. Try out your new life style for a few weeks while keeping your options open. Remember that you cannot escape from yourself and all your immediate problems merely by changing your locale.

## SUMMARY: THE COUNTERSTRESS
## PHILOSOPHY IN BRIEF
### Know your enemy
Identify the factors causing your distress. Unless you know what is producing your ulcer or putting your blood pressure up or keeping you awake at night you canot possibly take any lasting action to protect yourself. When the stress-inducing factors have been identified you can begin to take protective or evasive action. Eradicate the causes you can do without and shun those which can be avoided after deciding whether the advantages and benefits you obtain from stress-inducing activities outweigh the harmful effects they produce. Understand and learn to accept those factors which offer worthwhile benefits or which are vital or unavoidable.

### Know yourself
To understand precisely how environmental and personal pressures and strains affect your life you must understand your own motives, ambitions, habits and weak points. This doesn't require years of expensive and tiring psychoanalysis.

### Look for fulfilment
There are four areas in which you can achieve fulfilment: these are *home*, *work*, *hobby* and *friends*. If you obtain satisfaction from all four areas your ability to withstand pressures from the outside world will be enormous. The man or woman who has satisfaction from none of these areas is likely to suffer easily and often. The man or woman who invests and spends his or her intellectual capital wisely will receive good interest on the investment. All men and women need to extend the responsibility

they accept to fit their requirements. When work offers little responsibility or need for intellect then a leisure activity can provide both.

To survive, fight only the important battles and ignore the trivial ones. If your job is demanding ignore the attempts to persuade you to give your time to local politics or charitable organizations. They may be enough to take your stress level into the unbearable areas. Develop skills and talents in your work sufficient to make your services respected and required. To be needed is not far from being loved. To be loved is to be vaccinated against stress.

**Prepare a defence strategy**
Physical fitness is vital. Eat properly, exercise frequently and avoid tobacco. Learn how to relax and you will provide yourself with an excellent and long-lasting defence against the numerous strains of modern life.

Plan holidays well in advance and see that the plans are not changed at the last moment by business problems. Allocate time for rest and hobbies. If you work evenings and weekends then give yourself one afternoon a week when you are 'free to do your own thing'. This goes for the housewife as well as the man or woman who goes out to work. Insist that your free afternoon is sacrosanct and that whatever you choose to do you are not interrupted. Your work will improve as a result. It is far better to work in short sharp bursts than to work in long, tiring and tiresome sessions.

List-making often helps cut down pressure. Write down everything you have to do each day and you may find that the putting down on paper of your troubles is therapeutic. Keep a notebook with you to lighten the pressure on your memory. If you are planning a major move or some other event keep a page in your notebook on which to jot down ideas and thoughts. When a move of house is planned, for example, a carefully made list can ensure that everything goes smoothly by allowing plenty of time for things to be done. Waiting until the week before to contact the electricity company, the mail company, the newspaper delivery boy, the milk man and the printer for the new letterheads only adds to the inevitable problems.

Remember that being forewarned is being forearmed since if you know what problems the future has in store you can make the necessary plans.

Do not be frightened to let your emotions show occasionally. It is usually regarded as weak to display any sign of emotion in modern Western society. Men, in particular, are expected to hide their feelings completely. Nothing is more harmful than bottling up your emotions. When things go wrong it is far healthier to enjoy or endure a short sharp burst of anger or tears than it is to suffer silently and painfully for hours. Sufferers sit and seethe; survivors fume and then forget. The Swiss have now introduced a service enabling telephone subscribers to abuse specially prepared operators for £5 a minute. If you do not live in Switzerland it might help to smash a plate or two or visit a fairground and spend a few pennies on the Aunt Sally or coconut shy stalls. You might invest in a punchball. Be prepared to let your emotions hang out occasionally.

**Remember that attack is the best form of defence**
Protest when you disagree or disapprove with things being done on your behalf by politicians and bureaucrats. Join organizations protecting the environment and looking after the interests of the consumer if these subjects interest you. Do not become involved if you don't feel committed and avoid accumulating excessive secretarial responsibilities for organizations you join. Frustrations can often be eased by making your voice heard. And remember that many apparently final decisions have been reversed because of the noise made by protestors. If your protests are honest and well-intentioned your exposure to stress will be reduced by your participation.

**Finally**
Analyse your life style, change your life if necessary, choose your stress level. This is the most effective and efficient way to cope with the stresses and strains you will encounter in your life. If the stresses and strains you encounter are the ones you have chosen to face then they will be less damaging than if they are

the pressures you face reluctantly. And if the stresses you accept and choose promise to help you fulfil ambitions then the harmful effects they have will be minimal.

Although I have made this point several times in this book I think it is worth repeating that stress is an essential part of anyone's life. The trick is to try and ensure that you endure stresses which you find justifiable. Writing a book produces many stresses but the result is worth the effort. Studying at night school or training in the gymnasium produce pressures but offer participants rewards.

It is also worth remembering that if you do not want to opt out of the problems your style of life produces permanently then you should be prepared to ease yourself out of the hot seat you occupy every once in a while. A one week vacation every six months may be sufficient to keep you sane and healthy. An occasional weekend away may help. The cost of such excursions can be compared very favourably with the cost of spending two weeks in hospital while recovering from a heart attack or ulcer operation. I believe that the cost of all genuine holidays should be tax deductible.

Remember that the advantage of the counterstress philosophy over other recommended remedies is that it can do you no harm. You can only benefit from it. The benefits you enjoy will depend upon the sincerity with which you follow the guidelines of the philosophy.

# Part Three
## The Diseases Caused by Stress

In this section you will find descriptions of a large number of symptoms and problems caused by stress. There is a list of them on pages 114-116, so that you can look up any that are troubling you.

# INTRODUCTION

Sufferers from stress do not show a clearly defined specific set of symptoms. On the contrary there are innumerable different ways in which the human body may respond to a continued exposure to stress. Some patients exhibit primarily physical symptoms when subjected to excessive amounts of stress; others report less precise symptoms complaining of such abstract concepts as depression and anxiety. Mild headaches, insomnia and indigestion are simply the early physical signs of stress affecting the human body. Long-lasting stress results in the development of more important life threatening disorders.

It is not possible to say precisely how many people have died because of the effects of stresses as opposed to the effects of eating the wrong foods, smoking too much or taking too little exercise but all these causative factors inter-react and there is no doubt that stresses and strains arising from problems at work or at home play an important part in the build up of a heart attack. Despite the introduction of many new techniques for dealing with heart disorders the death toll from heart disease increases each year. Similarly more and more men in their fifties are suffering fatal strokes. The British Foreign Secretary, Anthony Crosland, died at the age of fifty-eight after a stroke said to have been brought on by overwork. It is certainly true that high blood pressure causes strokes and that stress causes high blood pressure.

The effects of stress on the body are so far-reaching that no organs remain unaffected and there are few diseases which are not made worse by stress. Tension and anxiety produce physiological changes in the body and those changes are in the long run often harmful. Even where there is no direct relationship between the effects of stress and a particular disease process we must remember that the body has to operate as a whole; and the adverse effects which produce changes in the cardiovascular system, for example, must inevitably have an effect on the body's capacity for dealing with disorders which cannot themselves be blamed on exposure to stress or strain.

In the pages which follow I have described some of the diseases most commonly associated with stress. I have explained why external stresses have an effect and given practical advice and information about how best to deal with the associated symptoms.

## SYMPTOMS AND DISEASES

Accidents 117
accident proneness 117
acrophobia 180
addiction 117
agoraphobia 180
aichmophobia 180
ailurophobia 180
alcoholism 119
allergic asthma 123
allergic dermatoses 123
allergic rhinitis 123
alopecia 139
anaemia 147, 150
angina pectoris 126
ankylosing spondylitis 185
anorexia 129
anthropophobia 180
antidepressants 152, 174
anxiety 131
aphthous ulcers 133
appetite 129
apoplexy 189
aquaphobia 180
arrythmia 134
arteriosclerosis 168
arthritis 185
asthma 135

Backache 137
baldness 139
barbiturate poisoning 61
battered babies 140
bed wetting 141
bereavement 6, 149
blood pressure 167
brantophobia 180
breasts (sore or swollen) 174
breathlessness 135
bronchitis 136

Cancer 195
cancerophobia 180
cardiac failure 161
cerebral arteriosclerosis 189
cerebral haemorrhage 189

cerebral thrombosis 189
cholecystitis 80
cholesterol 80, 169
claudication, intermittent 87
claustrophobia 180
cold, common 142
colitis, mucous 144
colitis, ulcerative 147
coma 156
constipation 80, 147
cough 87, 119
crying 151
cyesis 183
cynophobia 180
cystitis 148

Death 6
demophobia 180
depression 149
dermatitis 153
diabetes 155
diarrhoea 157
digestive disorders 172
dizziness 170
drugs 117, 132
duodenal ulcer 196
dysmenorrhoea 174
dyspepsia 172
dyspnoea 135

Eating problems 129, 177
eczema 153
eneuresis 141
epilepsy 158
equinophobia 180

Failing marriage 50, 187
faints 132
fat 177
fear 131
fever, hay 123
flatulence 80
frigidity 187

Gall bladder disease 80

gall stones 80
gastritis 196
gastroenteritis 157
giddiness 170
gout 185
'grand mal' 158

Habituation 117
haematemesis 199
hair loss 139
hay fever 123
headaches 160
heart attack 161
heart block 134
heart failure 161
heartburn 172
hepatitis 149
herpetophobia 180
homosexuality 187
hypertension 167
hypochondriasis 149
hysteria 132

Impotence 171
incontinence 141, 158
indigestion 172
infarction 162
infective diseases 142
infective hepatitis 149
influenza 142
insomnia 172
intermittent claudication 87
irritability 151, 174
ischaemic heart diseases 161
itching 123

Joint diseases 185

Kainophobia 180

Libido loss 180, 187
lumbago 137

Malignancy 195
marriage problems 50, 187
masturbation 187
melaena 199

memory failure 180
menopause 175
menstruation 174
migraine 175
mucous colitis 144
myocardial infarction 161
mysophobia 180
myxoedema 194

Nausea 200
nervous breakdown 131
nightmares 177
nyctophobia 180

Obesity 177
obsessions 177
obsessional behaviour 178
ophidophobia 180
osteoarthritis 185
overwork 179

Palpitations 180
peptic ulcer 196
personality disorders 43, 149
'petit mal' 158
phobias 180
phonophobia 180
poisoning 183
'post baby blues' 184
pregnancy 183
premenstrual tension 174
pruritus 123
psoriasis 183
puerperal depression 184
pyrophobia 180

Reactive depression 149
remedial exercises 189
respiratory diseases 135
retirement 51
rheumatic fever 185
rheumatoid arthritis 185

School phobia 180
sciatica 137
sexual problems 187
shortness of breath 135

sickness 200
siderodomophobia 180
sleeplessness 172
smoker's cough 87
stammer 190
status asthmaticus 135
stroke 189
stuttering 190
suicide 191

Tension 131
thanatophobia 180
tremors 195
tumours 195
thyroid troubles 194
thyrotoxicosis 194

Ulcer, aphthous 133
ulcer, duodenal 196
ulcer, gastric 196
ulcer, peptic 196
ulcerative colitis 147
urinary disease 148
urinary infections 148

Viruses 142, 149
vomiting 176, 197, 200

Wheezing 135

Xenophobia 180

Zoophobia 180

## Accident proneness

We usually think of accidents as unforeseen and unforeseeable events occurring purely by chance. There is, however, a good deal of evidence to show that accidental injuries are not always completely unpredictable and that not all accidents are caused by bad luck alone.

In many cases, of course, an accidental injury results from carelessness or stupidity. The motorist who crashed while driving on bald tyres in fog at seventy miles an hour is partly responsible for his own 'accident'. The building worker who refused to wear a safety helmet and then suffers a fractured skull when a piece of piping falls on to his head is not simply out of luck.

On numerous other occasions, however, accidents occur because of the victim's state of mind as much as his ill fortune. Many studies have shown that accident victims were often worrying about problems at home or at work when injured. Obviously the man who is worrying about his job will be a dangerous driver; the woman worrying about her husband's infidelity is likely to be careless when handling the washing machine. Children often respond to problems at home by being more restless, more aggressive, more daring and more adventurous than their contemporaries. If accommodation at home is inadequate, father unemployed and mother ill then the children will be rebellious and attention-seeking.

Chronic accident victims who are rarely without sutures or plaster of Paris casts should perhaps ask themselves whether or not their injuries are caused simply by ill fortune or are perhaps simply symptoms of long-lasting stresses and strains. The accident prone patient might be better off trying to adapt to or change his environment than putting his faith in horseshoes and rabbits' feet.

## Addiction

Each year a great deal of effort and a great deal of money are spent on trying to help people thought to be dependent on or addicted to a way of life that non-dependent, non-addicted people believe to be harmful. The help that is offered comes in

117

many different forms; depending, of course, upon the nature of the addiction and the disposition of the good samaritan. The three words addiction, dependence and habituation are frequently used to describe the affection people feel for their chosen means of support. Doctors try to give the words individual meaning by grading addicts as suffering from a physiological need, dependents as being merely psychologically stuck on their saving vice and the remaining sufferers as simply having an unfortunate habit.

Addicts, dependents and those with bad habits will have probably all noticed that what is one man's vice may be another man's recreation and that what may to a victim be a sign of degradation may to a saviour be necessary support. The alcoholic may despise those who survive through the use of drugs. The junkie may despise the alcoholic. The good samaritan who struggles to save them both may be addicted to tobacco. The smoker may be the object of the attentions of a saviour hooked on Valium.

What seems to have gone unnoticed is the fact that the human organism seems doomed to dependence on something. Whether that something is tobacco, alcohol, heroin, Valium or gambling it is an essential part of life. The human organism, it seems, is unable to survive without some sort of artificial crutch.

Long before the pressures of modern living were first described there were methods of support available for those too bored, too weak or too harassed to cope without them. Opium in its many forms has for centuries been a popular means of escape, as has alcohol. Religion has for thousands of years provided millions with support. Today the television set provides an easy way out of what may otherwise be a tedious existence. It provides the lonely with company, the bored with thrills and the over-excited with a soporific.

The similiarity between the various forms of addiction has been largely overlooked. Nevertheless it seems to me to be a fact that people smoke, drink, gamble, watch television, inject themselves and swallow pills for much the same reason. The human organism is basically frail and spiritually slight. Support, in whatever form, is an essential part of life for many people. If then we need some form of addiction to see us through life is there any point at all in spending time and money on attempts to wean addicts away from their support? Surely the alcoholic will take to tobacco or gambling, the junkie will become dependent upon prescribed pills and the gambler will become a religious fanatic. Good samaritans will point out that some forms of addiction are more harmful than others and that all people should be encouraged to choose the least harmful crutch. That is, in theory, a fine argument but who is to say just which addiction is the least harmful? Alcohol destroys the liver, tobacco ruins the lungs, television affects the mind, gambling results in ruin and poverty. The non-prescribed drugs have well-publicized dangers as do the prescribed drugs. Even religion has its dangers as many citizens around the world would readily confirm.

There is no way in which any one of us can determine which is the least harmful form of support to adopt; if only because we are all biased observers. This book will, however, help addicts, dependents and those with harmful habits see why they need support and how best they can reorganize their lives so as to reduce their need for an artificial crutch of any kind.

## Alcoholism

Most alcoholics aren't tramps living rough and swigging methylated alcohol from empty wine bottles. They are successful people in their middle years who have for years been struggling unsuccessfully to control a drinking habit which began as a social activity and gradually got out of hand. According to figures published by the British government there are estimated to be about half a million alcoholics in England and Wales alone. Many are single, widowed or divorced. Most are in their forties or fifties. Commercial travellers, successful businessmen, publicans, waiters, hoteliers, seamen, actors and doctors are the most likely candidates for the disease. Commonly the alcoholic will be either unusually shy and nervous or exceptionally gregarious and always eager for company. Many alcoholics have unhappy home lives. Inevitably a great many of the people who take to alcohol do so to help relieve their tensions and anxieties since alcohol acts as a tranquillizer.

Alcoholism is truly an international disease. It is said that ninety per cent of all addiction problems around the world concern people who are addicted to alcohol. In France each man, woman and child averages 110 litres of wine, 40 litres of beer and about 2½ litres of spirits every year, although the French National Academy of Medicine has recently published details of what it considers to be a sensible and restrained total daily intake of alcohol, they suggest that a man in good health should not drink more than three quarters of a litre of wine a day. The Dutch spend less than anyone on alcohol though their consumption is not inconsiderable – the average person gets through 4 litres of wine a year, 45 litres of beer and 2 litres of spirits. The Czechs and the Poles on the other hand spend about ten per cent of their annual income on alcohol (probably because it is more expensive in their country) and in both these countries people consume more alcohol than the British who spend on average only about four or five per cent of their annual incomes on alcohol. None spend as much as the people of Yugoslavia who spend up to nineteen per cent of their national income on alcohol.

All these figures appeared in a survey produced by the World Health Organization. The survey, entitled *Problems and Programmes related to alcohol and drug dependence in 33 countries*, also included information on drinking habits and trends. In the wine-producing countries of southern Europe much of the intake goes down with meals – for wine is an ordinary accompaniment to a meal. In beer-consuming countries alcohol is often consumed in pubs, as in Britain. In Poland the most popular drink is vodka (hence their heavy consumption of spirits) and most vodka is drunk in bars and restaurants. American habits are predictably cosmopolitan.

The results produced by this massive consumption of alcohol are not always pleasant or expected. In France the proportion of alcoholic patients in hospitals is between 25 per cent and 45 per cent on male wards. No less than 37 per cent of admissions to mental hospitals in France are patients with alcoholic problems. In Australia where the average intake of beer is 228 litres 20 to 40 per cent of hospital admissions are patients with alcoholic problems.

Alcoholic consumption is also closely related to vagrancy and criminal offences. A large proportion of the vagrants in all countries have alcohol problems and figures show that many of those in prison have problems with drinking. In Chile in 1969 30 per cent of all arrests were for drunkenness. Excessive alcoholic intake is said to be the cause of about 30 per cent of road accidents in France, and in Australia, where the death rate from traffic crashes is now five times as great as that from all infectious diseases put together, alcohol consumption is known to be the principal factor behind at least 50 per cent of road deaths. In Chile 70 per cent of males involved in traffic accidents have a blood alcohol level of over 100 mg per 100 ml. In Zambia 55 per cent of traffic accident victims had blood alcohol levels of over 150 mg per 100 ml. In Switzerland tests on over 1,000 people injured in road traffic accidents showed that one third had been under the influence of alcohol.

The past twenty years have seen an increase in per capita consumption for the British population aged fifteen and over as follows:

|          | 1955        | 1976        |
|----------|-------------|-------------|
| Beer     | 181.2 pints | 269.9 pints |
| Wine     | 3.4 pints   | 14.0 pints  |
| Spirits  | 3.1 pints   | 8.5 pints   |

One of the enormous problems associated with alcoholism is that it is extremely difficult to define the disease and to describe exactly what an alcoholic is, how much he drinks and what his precise symptoms are. The doctor who replied that an alcoholic is anyone who drinks more than I do wasn't being altogether jocular for undoubtedly the definition is one that many would use. Another problem is that according to Dr William H. Crosby (writing in the *Journal of the American Medical Association*, July 1977) the alcoholic is, in most cases, in trouble ten years before he is forced to seek help through illness.

Clearly it is vital to be able to define with some accuracy the symptoms of early alcoholism. Since the drinker is unlikely to be prepared to admit that he might have a problem the responsibility for spotting an early alcoholic usually rests with the relatives and friends.

Heartburn and indigestion (see p. 171) are two of the commonest early symptoms. It is said that alcoholics are amongst the best customers of companies making antacids. The stomach contains acid which is strong enough to burn holes in your carpet and yet it will complain if too much alcohol is poured into it. Rich foods, cigarette smoke and alcohol are all causes of heartburn and indigestion.

An indigestion type of pain which doesn't go away and which goes through to the back may herald an attack of pancreatitis. The pancreas is a vitally important gland which is situated near to the duodenum and which not only produces the hormone insulin, so important in the breakdown and usage of sugar, but also produces many of the important enzymes which aid digestion. Pancreatic pains are often relieved when the sufferer leans forward. The only real cure for the condition is abstinence.

Patients with a drinking problem may also begin coughing in the early morning. Since alcoholics are also often smokers the cough may be put down to smoker's cough. Palpitations (see p. 180), headaches (see p. 160) and tremor (see p. 195) are also symptoms of heavy drinking. Bruises which appear as a result of falls may be difficult to explain away. Finally of course alcoholics will often complain of insomnia. The nightcap they take to try and relieve this particular problem simply adds to the insomnia.

There are several 'social' symptoms which may help give away the drinker who is in danger. When entertaining he'll probably insist on pouring the drinks and may take a private taster before handing round the glasses. He'll stop at the bar when going into a restaurant and keep alcohol in the office as well as at home. There will be days lost from work, embarrassing incidents at parties and probably a lower sex drive. As the problems resulting from these affairs build up so will the need for alcohol. The man or woman who relieves pressure by drinking is starting on a route which has few slip roads. Early morning drinking is a final sign of the onset of alcoholism.

What can be done to help the alcoholic? The first thing is to persuade the drinker to accept his or her problem. Without that acceptance it is difficult if not impossible to do anything to help. Close relatives or friends can help by giving up drinking altogether themselves and by avoiding sharp comments when tonic water or tomato juice is ordered at a bar. Probably most important of all is to accept professional help. There are a number of clinics and hospitals which specialize in helping alcoholics. And, of course, there is the organization Alcoholics Anonymous, branches of which exist all around the world and membership of which provides support and companionship for the new abstainer. Occasionally an alcoholic may be encouraged to take tablets which produce a nauseous feeling if alcohol is taken at the same time.

It is worth adding that although alcohol causes many problems and much unhappiness it does have numerous valuable attributes. It is one of the most underestimated drugs available and for more than six thousand years healers have recorded its medicinal properties. Hippocrates was a great believer in wine as a medicine and the Bible contains many references to the miraculous properties of alcohol. Used sparingly and intelligently, treated with caution and respect, alcohol can be an important and useful medical aid. A small glassful of sherry used occasionally can provide a night's sleep, a dry white wine will often stimulate the appetite and in cardiovascular diseases (see pp. 161-171) alcohol may help to open up blood vessels.

## Allergies

A large proportion of any population will be allergic to something or other. Some people are allergic to foods (strawberries and lobsters are among the commonest) while others have allergies to drugs (penicillin is a frequent cause of allergic symptoms). Well-known household substances such as house dust, feather and nylon may also produce symptoms. Allergies to pollen, usually known by the term 'hay fever', are the best known type of allergy.

Similar symptoms develop with all allergies. The patient will usually complain of itching and of a rash. When the allergy is to something that is swallowed (such as a food or a drug) the

123

rash will cover the entire body. When the allergy is to something which attacks one specific part of the body (such as grass pollen) then the symptoms are likely to be related to that part of the body. Hay fever sufferers, for example, will usually complain of sneezing, of itching eyes and of a runny nose. This is because the pollen only affects them when it is breathed in through the nose. The 'rash' is confined to the nasal mucosa and the sneezing is caused by an itchiness inside the nose.

Some allergies are seasonal. Hay fever, for example, usually affects people only in the summer months. Other allergies last the year round. People who are allergic to dogs or cats or to particular materials, clothes or metals, may suffer in any season.

Most allergies are annoying rather than dangerous. Hay fever disrupts the warmer months for sufferers and makes summer examinations difficult. It doesn't usually put the sufferer at risk. There are, however, allergies which can kill. For example, patients who develop allergies to drugs may develop such exaggerated symptoms that their lives are at risk if they take just one tablet of the drug to which they're allergic. Some patients develop violent allergic reactions when bitten by wasps. Instead of a small itchy red lump their whole body reacts so violently that normal functions may be permanently interrupted.

The psychological influences which can contribute to the symptoms suffered by allergic patients have been well evaluated. It has been shown that people who are allergic to cats may develop their symptoms when shown photographs of cats and that hay fever sufferers who sneeze when in contact with flower pollen may sneeze when shown pictures of flowers. This lack of a genuine irritant does not mean that the symptoms are unreal; it simply means that the body has been tricked by the mind into reacting as though the stimulus were real. The sneeze which is produced by the hay fever sufferer is a normal defence mechanism produced to try and expel the source of the irritation – the pollen which has irritated the nasal mucosa. Normally if pollen is sucked into the nose a sufferer will sneeze in an attempt to dislodge it. The sneezing may well be far more enthusiastic than is really necessary because the reaction within the nose is excessive. When the sufferer is shown a photograph of a flower his body reacts instantly. It 'orders' a sneeze as an early defence mechanism. Threaten a man with a knife and he'll run if he can. He hasn't been cut or injured but he doesn't want to wait around to see if it's going to happen. He reacts before there is any direct stimulus.

Any reaction which can be triggered off by an emotional or mental stimulus rather than a physical stimulus is obviously going to be affected by strains and pressures. Anxiety and disquiet affects the body as well as the mind and a worried person will be both physically and mentally susceptible to new pressures. When under strain we are far less capable of coping with additional problems and we are likely to react too quickly to a stimulus. Our nerves are 'on edge'. Clearly, therefore, personal or environmental strains can contribute to the development of allergy symptoms.

There are a number of ways in which patients who suffer from allergies can be helped. The most common form of treatment involves the use of drugs called antihistamines.

When a trigger produces an allergy reaction the body's defence mechanisms include the production of a chemical called histamine. It is this substance which produces the skin irritation which leads to the development of the itchy rash so well known to all allergic sufferers. Antihistamines oppose the action of this chemical. They do this very effectively but unfortunately there is a problem: they also make many people drowsy. Fortunately there are dozens of different brands of antihistamine available and although it may necessitate experimenting with several different brands most people can eventually find an antihistamine which suits them and which helps to control their symptoms. As well as antihistamine tablets there are antihistamine drops for soothing itchy eyes and antihistamine injections to help relieve more severe bouts of itching.

Steroids are sometimes used in the treatment of allergic symptoms and the prevention of allergic reactions. Undoubtedly steroids, which have a general anti-inflammatory effect, can be very effective in dampening down the body's reactions to a stimulus but unfortunately they can cause dangerous, even fatal, side effects and should therefore only be used in the treatment of severe allergic reactions and even then should be used for short-term treatment only. Steroids are available both as tablets and as injections.

Some patients can be helped by a series of desensitizing injections. Tests are done to find out exactly what causes the patient's symptoms and then special injections are prepared which are given once a week for several months. These injections, which consist of gradually increasing but still very small doses of the substance to which the patient is allergic, and which help the body prepare for contact with the substance itself, will sometimes help keep the symptoms at bay for many months.

Because of the seriousness of the reactions which may occur when allergic patients become re-exposed to the stimuli to which they are allergic it is wise for those who have severe reactions to wear some sort of identification warning informing doctors and other first aid personnel of their allergy. The Medic Alert organization produces necklaces and bracelets which carry the owner's name and brief details of an important allergy. It is, for example, vital that a patient who is penicillin sensitive does not receive penicillin accidentally. The mistake could prove fatal.

### Angina Pectoris (see also heart attacks p. 161)

One of the commonest causes of death among men with young families is heart disease (see pp. 161–167). Anginal attacks are the early warning signs of heart disease. It is therefore vitally important that all adult men and all adult women are able to recognize an attack of angina. Unrecognized, the heart's condition can simply continue to deteriorate whereas if an anginal attack is recognized and action taken a heart attack can very probably be avoided.

The human heart is responsible for pumping blood around the body and for ensuring that all other organs and tissues receive a good supply of oxygenated blood. Blood brings food and takes away waste products. Naturally the heart muscles need to be kept supplied with fresh blood just like other muscles throughout the body. The arteries (called coronary arteries) which carry this blood are therefore doing a vitally important job. (The word coronary literally means encircling and is apt since the heart's arteries encircle it in the same way that a crown encircles the head.)

When the arteries supplying the heart are blocked, temporarily or permanently, partially or completely, the heart muscles are deprived of fresh blood. Since these compact, powerful muscles are expected to keep the heart pumping away approximately seventy times a minute they need a great deal of food and oxygen. They produce much waste and suffer badly if their supply system is at fault. The pain is caused by the shortage of oxygen and the accumulation of metabolic wastes. There are nerve receptors around the coronary arteries which react quickly if anything goes wrong with the blood supply. These nerve receptors send impulses off which produce a tight, constricting ache or pain usually said to be behind the breast bone. It may also be across the upper part of the chest, in the neck, jaw or arms. The pain usually comes in spasms. Hence the name angina pectoris. The word 'angina' suggests the spasmodic nature of the pain and the word 'pectoris' describes the area of the chest involved.

There are several reasons why the arteries supplying the heart may be blocked or narrowed. These are discussed in the section on heart attacks.

Since effort and exercise put a greater demand on the heart and result in an increased need for oxygen and a greater output of waste products from the muscles, angina pectoris is made worse by continued exercise. On the other hand when the body is at rest the strain on the heart decreases. Clearly, therefore, if a man or woman complains of a pain which resembles the pain of angina pectoris then they should immediately stop whatever they are doing and rest. Because anxiety and fear put a pressure on the body and produce an increased demand for blood in all parts of the body they also increase the pressure on the heart. The heart rate rises and the volume of blood distributed around the body also rises. Clearly, therefore, for exactly the same reasons that exercise is likely to increase the pain of angina pectoris anxiety, fear and other emotional conditions are likely to lead to more pain if a patient is suffering from angina.

In the short term then, when a patient complains of chest pain he should rest and be kept as free as possible of all worries and problems. In the long term the man or woman who has suffered from an attack of angina pectoris should be treated in just the same way as any patient with a heart condition. They should diet if overweight, take a moderate amount of gentle exercise, and avoid cigarettes. Large meals and cold weather are two other factors likely to produce the onset of anginal pain in a susceptible subject.

There are a number of drugs made for the aid and relief of angina sufferers. The most important drug is called glyceryl trinitrate. This is in itself an oily, non-inflammable liquid which is also known as nitroglycerin and which is a rather more powerful explosive than gunpowder. When mixed with an inert substance and turned into a tablet it becomes safe and very useful in the treatment of angina. It should be placed under the tongue and allowed to dissolve. Pain relief starts within a couple of minutes and the pill may be used to help prevent the onset of pain if unavoidable exercise is about to be taken.

Glyceryl trinitrate tablets produce a headache in many patients but usually this is far less fierce than the chest pain and is therefore acceptable. It is important to remember that these tablets do not last for more than a year. After that they lose their potency and need to be thrown away and replaced. Like all tablets they should be kept in a closed brown bottle since they deteriorate when exposed to heat or air. There are a number of other pills prescribed for patients with the symptoms of angina. None of them are as important or useful as glyceryl trinitrate.

Angina is an early warning sign. There is powerful evidence to suggest that patients with angina who have frustrating jobs, who are depressed by their work or home life and who cannot find real satisfaction in anything they do are likely to die suddenly and quickly of a heart attack if they do nothing and ignore the warning signs. There is now evidence that heart disease is often inherited. Dr Samuel A. Levine of Boston, published research in the *American Heart Journal* which showed that not only do sons often die of heart disease in the same way as their father did but that they showed signs and symptoms of heart trouble at a much younger age. Men whose fathers had presented with angina at the age of sixty are appearing with signs of angina at the age of forty. In fact the average age at the onset of symptoms of angina for twenty men was 61.2 years; their twenty-one sons showed symptoms of angina at an average age of 48.1 years. It seems likely, therefore, that modern life is more likely to lead to the development of heart disease. Men whose fathers suffered heart attacks should therefore be aware of the risk.

## Anorexia

Nothing worries the average mother more than finding that one of her loved ones is not eating well. Anxious mothers of all ages regularly appear in doctors' offices dragging with them husbands and offspring suspected of 'having gone off their food'. The technical medical term for a loss of appetite is 'anorexia' and there are many different causes responsible for this not uncommon problem.

The term 'anorexia' is itself usually linked popularly with another medical word 'nervosa'. Together these two words describe a condition in which the patient, usually a girl or young woman, cannot and will not eat at all. Anorexia nervosa is a mental condition which may become very serious. Most of the young women who develop this disorder are rather obsessional and may also be hysterical from time to time. Commonly these patients will have been plump as children and will have gone from one extreme to another as they have grown older. Their distaste for food is extraordinary and many will force themselves to vomit if they are persuaded to eat. The loss of weight which inevitably occurs is often considerable and may indeed prove fatal.

Anorexia resulting from anxiety (see p. 131) and worry is a much more common complaint. Like anorexia nervosa this is a loss of appetite caused by a mental condition but unlike anorexia nervosa it is usually short-lived and far from dangerous. Most people will remember days on which they were so excited or worried that swallowing food proved simply impossible. Ask a bride what she had to eat on her wedding day, ask a student what he had to eat on a day when he was taking an examination and you'll find that very little was swallowed! All sorts of emotions, ranging from depression and fear to anxiety and excitement cause a dryness of the mouth and result in a loss of appetite. It is as if the body decides that there are far more important things to be done than mere eating! Usually this condition lasts only hours or days. Occasionally it may persist and be associated with vague epigastric pains and a particular dislike of fried or fatty foods.

Patients with stomach lesions may also lose their appetites for far more practical reasons. For example, some types of peptic ulcer (see p. 196) result in the feeling of pain when food is swallowed. Inevitably, therefore, the patient with this type of ulcer is unlikely to want to eat. He knows that eating will cause pain. Patients with cancer of the stomach are also likely to lose their appetites and patients who have had part of their stomachs surgically removed as a treatment for ulceration usually find that their appetite diminishes accordingly. Again this can be explained by the fact that the body, realizing the stomach's diminished capabilities, is protecting it by dampening down the appetite.

Anorexia is also a problem with elderly people. The reasons are often as much social as medical. Elderly people often live alone and simply cannot be bothered to cook for themselves. They find the effort of buying and preparing food too much for them. In addition the elderly will have often lost their own teeth. Ill-fitting dentures may make eating difficult. It may make the digestion of tough foods such as steak totally impossible.

People who do not eat properly for long periods become weak, of course, and people who are weak usually have poor appetites. They cannot be bothered to eat and so they get weaker. The vicious circle gets tighter and tighter. Deficiencies of iron or vitamin C may result in sore mouths. People who take too little iron often get sore tongues and people whose intake of vitamin C is too small may develop cracked lips and sores at the corners of their mouths. Obviously eating for these people will be difficult and painful. They will eat less than they should, they will become weak and they will suffer more.

Any cook should know how to stimulate the appetite of her husband and her children. The anorexic patient will, more than any other person, need well-presented and attractive looking food. To try and stimulate his or her appetite make up a tray of food which contains some of his or her favourite dishes. Do not put too much on the plate at once for a surfeit of food may prove distressing to the patient with no appetite. Give plenty of drinks with food, make sure that food does not need a great deal of chewing or cutting. Easily swallowed foods are best. Jelly and blancmange, ice-cream and fruit and soups are among the best foods for people who have lost their appetite. Whatever you do try and keep cheerful if your carefully prepared plate of food is left only half eaten. Do not scold. Offer encouragement and then, when it is clear that nothing more will be eaten, remove the plate. Try and make sure that the smells of cooking do not pervade the house and clear away dirty dishes as soon as possible. Remember that anorexia at times of excitement is normal and fairly harmless.

## Anxiety

There are thousands of different causes of anxiety. An old lady may be anxious about her husband who is taken to hospital with a stroke. A young girl may be anxious about examination results. A football supporter may be anxious about his team's successes. A woman preparing a dinner party may anxiously await the arrival of her guests. Anxiety is a perfectly normal human response to crises, however minor those crises might appear to be to others.

Enduring some or all of these symptoms is part of life. If a man never had to put up with any of them he would be inhuman. Our society is complicated, unpredictable and contradictory; it is inevitable that there should be ample opportunity for the average citizen to exhibit signs of anxiety. Much anxiety, of course, is essential. Stage performers claim that a little stage fright, a little tension, helps improve the quality of the performance they give. But there is of course a time when the level of anxiety becomes unbearable and something has to be done to ameliorate the symptoms of anxiety. Too much anxiety destroys a performance.

The symptoms of anxiety vary a good deal from patient to patient. Some complain of tremors, dizziness, headaches, indigestion, sweating, dry mouths and insomnia. Others have palpitations, butterflies in their stomachs or nervous diarrhoea. Impotence, breathlessness, an inability to concentrate, hysteria, depression, phobias and nightmares are all symptoms exhibited by the anxious. Fidgeting, faints and muscle tension are additional signs.

There are a number of drugs available which can be used to help the over-anxious. Barbiturates (which I described on p. 61 as being potentially dangerous drugs unsuitable for general use) are general cerebral depressants which reduce activity in all parts of the brain. The benzodiazepines (see p. 62) on the other hand, are rather more specific – they act on parts of the brain concerned with transmitting messages. A third group of drugs, among which there are the beta blockers, have a peripheral effect. They block the effects of the adrenalin released in times of crisis, stopping the development of symptoms such as tremor, palpitations, muscle tension, nausea and sweating.

Inevitably there are side effects with all these drugs. The barbiturates may cause excessive drowsiness and are addictive. The benzodiazepines, such as Valium and Librium, may cause drowsiness, deformities in unborn children and even aggressive behaviour. And the beta blockers have been known to permanently damage various organs of the body.

A more final solution is destructive brain surgery (see p. 58). The surgeon removes those parts of the brain which are involved in the development of the symptoms of anxiety. To me this seems rather like treating an ingrowing toe nail by removing the foot but some psychiatrists and neurosurgeons find the practice acceptable.

It is possible to treat symptoms specifically, rather than attempting to prevent the development of symptoms. For example, indigestion (see p. 172) can be treated with an antacid.

The amelioration of symptoms can be therapeutic since the somatic symptoms of anxiety may re-inforce the psychological fears of the individual. The worried man with indigestion begins to worry about having an ulcer. He now has an extra problem and an extra pain. Treat his indigestion and you at least take him back to where he was before the pain started.

Naturally it is far more effective to teach the man or woman who suffers from attacks of anxiety how best to identify sources of anxiety and apprehension and how best to cope with them. Short-term solutions, such as drugs, have no lasting value. As the old Chinese proverb says, 'Give a man fish and you feed him for a day, teach him how to catch fish and you feed him for a lifetime'. In the most severe panic attacks victims should learn to breathe deeply and count slowly. Controlling respiratory movements is particularly important since then the body is kept more or less under control.

**Aphthous ulcers**
Aphthous ulcers are infuriating. They are minute and often hardly visible and yet they cause excrutiating pain and can be as annoying and tiresome as may more obvious lesions. They usually form in the cheeks, under the tongue or on the inner side of the lower lip; they are white and rarely more than a couple of millimetres in diameter; they last on average for a week or ten days and they are painful when touched even lightly. They usually arrive in packs of three or four.

No one knows exactly what causes the development of aphthous ulcers but some people are definitely more susceptible than others. Those who get aphthous ulcers are likely to have them at irregular intervals for most of their lives, from their early teens until middle age. They usually occur more irregularly in later life.

Although physical traumas (slipping with the toothbrush or chewing something particularly hard) may seem to produce aphthous ulcers the most important causative factor is undoubtedly distress. Many treatments are available but none of them are universally successful. Most of the treatments your doctor can prescribe can be bought from a pharmacist.

### Arrhythmias of the heart

Most hearts beat between 60 and 80 times a minute and usually the time interval between beats is the same length. Sometimes, however, the heart beats irregularly and instead of there being a heart beat every second or so there may be one beat in a second followed by two beats in the next second, and so on.

There are many reasons why this happens. Hormonal diseases such as thyrotoxicosis (an excess of thyroid hormone (see p. 194) may be responsible and there are many different types of heart disease which produce arrhythmias of the heart. In heart failure, for example, when the heart is beginning to find its daily work a little too much for it the pulse may be fast and irregular as the heart beats away trying to catch up with its work. After a heart attack (see p. 161) the damaged heart may beat irregularly.

It is, however, extremely common for all of us to have slight irregularities in our pulse even though our hearts and hormones may be working perfectly. Odd additional beats occur quite frequently and seem to be particularly noticeable at night and after exercise. Tired, overstressed people get extra heart beats as do some people after drinking coffee or alcohol or smoking tobacco. Usually these extra beats disappear when the patient exercises.

It is not a good idea, however, to see if your extra heart beats disappear when you run up the stairs to the top of a sixteen-storey building. Even if you do not have any symptoms of illness see your doctor for a check up. He may think that you are making a bit of a fuss but you can always blame me.

Once your extra beats have been officially diagnosed as harmless you can chase the neighbour's cat round the garden to get rid of them.

A patient who complains of an irregularly beating heart may need to have an electrocardiogram. This investigation is likely to be conducted on any patient with any sort of notable heart condition. Leads are attached to the patient's body and the electrical impulses which are fired off within the heart are recorded by the machine on a long strip of paper. Electrocardiography is one of the more useful investigations available to modern doctors and with the aid of the long strip of paper and a lot of experience the doctor conducting the test can find out a great deal about his patient's heart. Hospital in-patients, particularly those who have had heart attacks or who are suspected of having had heart attacks are likely to find themselves wired up to one of these machines semi-permanently. The tracing will then not be recorded for posterity on a piece of paper but will appear on a small screen where it can be studied by doctors, nurses and inquisitive visitors. These machines usually emit some sort of attention-catching noise if there is any interruption in the regular supply of heart beats and patients who are lonely will find that simply pulling out one of the small plugs at the back of the machine will produce a sudden influx of visitors.

## Asthma

Allergies (see p. 123), infections and psychological problems are the three main causes of asthma and the associated wheezing and breathlessness.

The many allergy factors which may cause asthma include dust and pollen. Certain types of animals may also be responsible and a household pet may prove to be the cause of repeated attacks of asthmatic wheezing. Pillows filled with feathers may also cause asthma. There are a number of ways of cutting down asthma attacks caused by allergens. Firstly, it is essential to separate the sufferer from the trigger allergen. If the asthma is caused by dust or pollen then it may be necessary to keep the house clear of flowers in the summer, to keep the windows closed and to use the electric fan to help to keep the rooms cool. If a household pet is the cause then do not replace it when it dies. It is rarely wise to have a household pet put down for apart from the question of the animal's rights this can be most upsetting for children. When foodstuffs cause asthma then the solution is obvious.

If the allergen which causes asthma can be identified for a specific patient then even if it is impossible to separate the victim from the cause a special series of injections may be helpful and may provide temporary immunity. Steroid injections are also used occasionally to provide long-lasting relief. Both these methods of treatment can be hazardous and are only used when vital.

Infection can cause attacks of asthma which cannot be avoided or forecast. It is rarely practicable to keep a child out of contact with all sources of potential infection. All that can be done is to treat any infection as soon as it starts. Doctors sometimes give asthma sufferers a supply of antibiotics so that they can begin treatment themselves at the first sign of an infection.

The third cause of asthma is psychological. The close relationship between pressure, problems, strain, excitement and unhappiness and attacks of asthma is well documented. Anything which heightens emotional responses is likely to produce an attack of wheezing in a susceptible patient. Asthmatics often benefit from a change of human as well as external environment, showing that relationships with other people as well as atmospheric pollutants may be responsible for initiating attacks. Children are particularly likely to respond to difficulties in their relationships with other people by developing symptoms of asthma. The child whose mother is overprotective or whose father shows love irregularly and unpredictably is particularly likely to suffer from disturbed breathing. Parents who are anxious about and who worry about their child's health and are obsesssive about avoiding dangers and sources of infection can make a child so worried and apprehensive that asthma gets worse. To avoid fears like this the asthmatic child should be encouraged as much as he or she possibly can to fit in with other children.

When young children develop asthma there is often a family history of an allergic disease. Either mother or father or perhaps an uncle or grandparent will have had hay fever (see p. 123), migraine (see p. 175), eczema (see p. 153) or asthma. When older patients develop asthma there is frequently a past medical history of bronchitis. The symptoms in all cases are caused by a spasm and narrowing of the tubes which carry air into the lungs; this narrowing is made worse by an accumulation of sticky secretions in the lungs. The precise pathways by which these changes take place are complex and variable.

There are many different types of treatment available for asthmatics. Pressured aerosols which deliver drugs designed to relieve broncho-spasm used to be very popular but there have been many deaths caused by these aerosols. When used properly the risk is slight but many people find the temptation to over-use the sprays irresistible. Steroids are useful in emergencies and antibiotics may, of course, be necessary to help clear up infections. Parents and relatives can usually help by giving fluids. Rapid breathing and sweating means that fluid is lost and must be replaced.

Encouragement and support will also prove helpful. The asthmatic patient will recover more quickly if the surroundings are calm and peaceful. Panic spreads and relatives or friends who panic will make the asthmatic patient worse.

## Backache

Lumbago or low back pain is often something of a mystery disease for doctors and patients. Occasionally a prolapsed inter-vertebral disc or a torn spinal ligament may be found to be responsible. More often, however, no direct cause can be found. The patient will simply complain of sudden onset of low back pain which is made worse by movement and relieved by lying flat.

Although the precise cause of the pain may be unknown it is common for the back muscles of a patient with backache to be in spasm; they are contracted and tense. This is why strains of a mental or emotional nature are sometimes responsible for the development of backaches. When under strain, muscles of the body are tensed. If the tensed muscles are in the head then a headache results; if they are in the back then a backache develops.

More than half of all adults have backache at some time or another. People in their forties and fifties are most at risk but back pains are said to cost Britain about £200 million a year in lost work and sickness payments and on any day 50,000 British men and women will be off work with back pain. In a single calendar year 1½ million people will visit their doctors for treatment of backache.

137

The man or woman who is tense and under strain and whose muscles are kept taut and tight will much more easily damage them or more vital bony structures. Normally the muscles of the back are responsible for holding all cartilaginous and ligamentous structures comfortably. When tensed, muscles do not work efficiently; slight mechanical pressures can result in damage that would not normally be caused without much greater pressures.

Low back pain which is not accompanied by pains in the legs or feet will usually respond well to a few days rest in bed followed perhaps by some physiotherapy. Light exercise, massage and warmth will all relieve pain and spasm. Pills, particularly aspirin or paracetomol should help relieve pain and inflammation in the early stages. There is not very much point in calling your doctor unless you have fallen and feel you may have broken or damaged a bone in your spine. If the back pain is accompanied by pains in the legs it is possible that a nerve root may be irritated by a slipped or prolapsed disc. If this is the case treatment may take longer. Manipulation by an osteopath, physiotherapist or doctor may help as long as there is no physical damage to the spine. Manipulation of a spine with a prolapsed disc may make things worse.

To avoid a bad back it is wise to sit comfortably on comfortable chairs. Car seats are often badly designed and drivers who find that their backs ache after long journeys should invest in more acceptable car furniture if they wish to avoid further trouble. Check when buying a motor car that the front seats (which will be used most) are fully adjustable and firmly comfortable. Another cause of backache in motorists could well be the feeling of frustration which often rises up when a motorist is kept trapped in his steel cocoon in a traffic jam. This feeling of frustration tenses the muscles of the back and produces backache or lumbago.

When lifting heavy objects bend the knees and lift with the back straight. Immediately after the onset of any symptoms of backache avoid lifting, straining, pushing or pulling. It is important to keep the back muscles supple and pliable by ridding the body of tension and pressure as quickly as possible.

## Baldness

Every single hair on your head has its own root. A root which was present when you were born and which periodically becomes active and produces a visible hair. Not all hair roots produce hair at the same time and for a variety of reasons a number of roots may stop producing hairs. In the ordinary young, healthy adult, some hair roots will be in an active phase (producing hairs) while others will be in a resting phase (not producing any hairs). In older people, particularly men, more roots will be resting and consequently the scalp will be less liberally supplied with hair. The man is then said to be balding or suffering from alopecia. Both men and women tend to lose their hair as they age, and the loss of hair is related not to the amount of brushing it receives, the wearing of a hat, the type of shampoo used, the climate or any other similar factor. It is genetically determined. In other words, you have about as much control over whether or not you go bald as you have over whether you are six feet tall or five feet tall.

Baldness which is genetically determined usually affects men and begins with a thinning of the hair above the temples and on the top of the head and then gradually spreads over the scalp. There is often a good growth of hair around the sides and the back and vainer men may try to hide their baldness by combing long hair across the central bald patch.

The type of alopecia which causes most problems is, however, not this gradual thinning but a more dramatic hair loss which affects both men and women and which is known as alopecia areata. It occurs at any age but is most common in people in their teens and twenties. Instead of a slow loss of hair from the temples there is a sudden and fast loss in patches all over the scalp. The patches may coalesce and give the patient a completely bald head à la Kojak. The rate at which the hair falls out can be judged from the fact that on a normal healthy scalp hair falls out at the rate of between sixty and ninety hairs a day. In alopecia areata hair really does come out in handfuls. Even the eyebrows may disappear. The roots just stop growing for a while.

The precise cause of alopecia areata is unknown but in many

cases it is caused by worry or emotional strain. Patients with this complaint usually grow a fresh head of hair although this may take weeks or even months. In the meantime a wig can usually provide social cover.

Because hair has always been an important part of our appearance there have always been many people anxious to treat varying degrees of baldness with magical cures. Unfortunately there is still no cure for baldness (although at the time of writing a substance called dinitrochlorbenzole (DNCB) is being tested in Germany) and the man who has lost his hair is wasting his money if he buys creams or lotions to apply to his pate. The only way in which these substances can appear to work is by coincidence. Occasionally a patient using one of these treatments will get better automatically, and quite by chance. Nevertheless, he will give the treatment the benefit for his recovery.

Wigs or false hair pieces have been popular for centuries. Many men and women use wigs today, simply to provide a change in appearance which does not necessitate expensive and lengthy visits to a hairdresser. Others, who have lost some or all of their hair, rely upon wigs to replace their losses. Those who need hair pieces for psychological support can usually obtain them from their doctor (certainly in Britain wigs are available under the NHS), but the best and most skilfully made are available only on the commercial market. It is even possible these days to have a hair graft. Plastic surgeons will move hair from the neckline to the temples, thereby turning a balding man into a hirsute man – with a head of his very own hair!

### Battered babies

The battered baby syndrome is now, I'm afraid, a common occurrence in medicine. Most doctors will, at some time or another, have seen such a problem.

It is very difficult to make a firm diagnosis in these cases, for often the child will be brought to the doctor by a parent who tells a story of some accidental injury. One is naturally hesitant to suggest that he or she is lying.

Of course, there are no such problems when the child has broken bones and bad bruises spread about in such a way that violence has obviously been done. The most difficult cases occur when injuries are slight and apparently accidental. In such cases, the doctor must keep on his toes if he is to ensure that things don't get worse. At the same time, he must tread very carefully in order to avoid offending the innocent patient. At times like this, the rest of the doctor's team has a vital part to play. The social worker and the health visitor can make discreet enquiries and can help doctor and parents ensure that no further accidents occur.

Relatives and friends who notice that a child seems to get more than his fair share of bruises should perhaps ask themselves whether one, or both, of the parents are for some reason or other treating the child roughly. It is much easier to find out at this stage what is happening than it is to try and sort out the situation when a baby has been severely batttered. At the same time, it's important to avoid jumping to conclusions!

And, remember, all of us could, at some time or other, find ourselves hitting a child. It may have cried continually for hours, it may have kept us awake for several nights. Few of those who batter babies are cruel. Most just find things too much for them, are worried by outside problems and are just unable to cope with the naughty child. Do not be too quick to condemn – but do offer genuine help if you think it is needed.

### Bed wetting

Persistent bed wetting is a very common problem although no mother who has had to wash sheets half a dozen times in a week will think that the problem is anything but exceptional. One child in seven is still wetting the bed at the age of seven and although there are occasionally anatomical causes or infections which produce the eneuresis (the technical term for bed wetting) the common cause is worry or fear allied to a well developed bad habit.

Any child who is bed wetting at the age of six or older needs reassurance and help rather than admonishment and punishment. There are a few simple things which should be done to help. Make sure that the child goes to the lavatory last thing at night before he gets into bed, that he drinks nothing for two hours before going to bed and that he is lifted out of bed for a visit to the lavatory when his parents go to bed.

It is psychologically more helpful to congratulate the child on having a 'dry' night than to admonish him when he has 'wet' nights. Encouragement by making a list of the 'dry' nights or simply by showing obvious pleasure will do more good than frightening the child by making a list of the 'wet' nights; spanking him or showing him up will only contribute to the problem. The bed wetting child is often worried about something and the more he is told off the more he will worry and the worse he will become.

It always helps to find out just what is worrying the child. Bullying at school, worrying about some undiscovered error and a feeling of not being wanted may all be responsible factors.

There are, incidentally, a number of gadgets available to help the bed wetting child. There are, for example, special undersheets which are attached to buzzers and which ring an alarm when moistened. Theoretically these alarms teach the child to recognize when the passage of urine is imminent.

Doctors occasionally prescribe drugs to make a child sleep less deeply and so ensure that they respond to a full bladder more quickly.

### Colds and flu
The common cold and the almost equally common influenza are today responsible for most of the days off work and days off school taken by people all around the world. Despite the progress that has been made in many areas of medicine doctors can still do very little about preventing colds or treating them. The scientific search for a cure for the common cold was started in 1926 by Dr Alphonse Dochez working in New York and in 1946 it was intensified when the British Medical Research Council set up a Common Cold Research Unit in Salisbury. Today, however, the man who helped set up the British Unit admits that it is unlikely that any cure will ever be found. It seems, therefore, that we must learn to live with colds and respiratory tract infections and to cope with them as best we can.

Many people seem confused by the terms 'cold' and 'flu' and

use them indiscriminately. In fact the symptoms of a common cold are far less fearsome than the symptoms of flu. The patient with a cold will usually complain of a streaming nose and of sneezing attacks. The patient with the more debilitating flu will, however, complain of sweating, headache, muscle aches and pains and a general feeling of great weakness. The patient with a cold can often struggle to work; the patient with flu will usually have great difficulty in dragging himself out of bed. Anyone under pressure is more susceptible to cold and flu viruses. These are very common stress diseases.

Both the common cold and the flu usually last for a week or so. Whether or not the flu or cold sufferer goes to work or stays at home depends upon several factors. It naturally depends upon just how bad the victim feels but it also depends on the type of work involved, the route to work and the feelings of the other people at work.

Naturally the man who works as a labourer on a building site will be better off at home if he has a really bad cold. The man who works alone in an office may be able to work fairly easily. The man whose job is twenty miles away will be less enthusiastic about going to work than the man who has to travel only a hundred yards. And the man who works in a busy office will be unpopular if he turns up!

By and large children can usually give their mums a good idea about whether or not they are fit to go to school themselves. The child with a cold should be fine for school as long as he is not sneezing too much but the child with a high temperature and general muscle pains will need to be, and want to be, kept at home.

Cold and flu victims who stay in the house should keep warm and drink plenty of warm drinks. Fruit squashes are probably the best types of drink but personally I always find that lemon tea by the pint is very refreshing. Food should be kept light and easy to eat and rest is essential although that does not mean staying in bed. Sitting downstairs in front of the fire and television set may be just as restful.

Aches and pains can be relieved by simple soluble aspirin or paracetomol tablets.

It is the complications of colds and flu which cause most problems. If the infection goes down on to the patient's chest and results in the development of a cough which brings up discoloured sputum then the doctor's advice should be sought. An antibiotic may be needed. Other symptoms which merit seeking professional advice include shortness of breath and the coughing up of blood. All these are symptoms of a deep chest infection.

The patient who complains after his cold has died down that he gets frontal headaches across his eyes has probably developed an infection of his sinuses. He should visit the doctor's surgery if the headache persists. A sore throat, a painful ear or an inability to speak all suggest that the infection has spread and become rather more serious. Of course, each of these three symptoms occur in mild form and for a couple of days during an ordinary attack of flu. It is only if these symptoms persist that professional advice is really needed.

Many patients ask about the value of flu injections. Now that aeroplanes fly all around the world in a matter of hours new types of flu virus are taken from one country to another quickly and an injection which gives immunity against one type of virus may not protect against another. However, it is still probably worthwhile patients with a susceptibility to chest infections or to infections of any kind having a flu jab in the autumn. The autumn is the best time not because flu and colds only affect patients in the winter (they don't) but because in the winter there is an increased chance of a patient developing complications. I only recommend flu jabs for the elderly, the diabetic or the bronchitic patients. I really do not think it is worth giving younger, comparatively healthy people, flu jabs.

Mothers, who usually get the job of nurse, when anyone has a cold or flu, should remember that these diseases are infectious and easily spread. Visitors should be kept to a minimum.

### Colitis

The average intestinal tract is about thirty feet long. Converting food into faeces and extracting the necessary nutrient from it is a complex and lengthy business; each portion of the intestine has its part to play. Every inch of that thirty feet can be influenced by the nervous system. It is nervous impulses which control the activity of the muscles of the bowel and which have authority over the glands which secrete digestive substances.

When environmental or psychological pressures on the human body become too great for comfort the nerves which control the intestines suffer excessive stimulation. The muscles of the bowel become tense and tight just as the muscles of the forehead or neck become tense. This means, of course, that the patient notices the effects of this change in muscle tone. Frustration, anxiety (see p. 131), fatigue and other problems result in the normal colonic contractions being far more intense and powerful than is usually the case. High pressure builds up inside the colon and the result can either be constipation (see p. 147) or diarrhoea (see p. 157). Commonly the patient notices diarrhoea in the early morning accompanied by the passing of mucus.

When it is the colon which suffers the brunt of the patient's pressures and shows the first signs of the stress threshold having been breached the initial symptoms are usually vague and inconclusive. Early morning diarrhoea may be accompanied by a little pain in the lower part of the abdomen, often on the left side. Later the pains may clear up and the diarrhoea may be replaced by constipation. Another problem which is often extremely embarrassing is the passing of vast quantities of wind. Occasionally this just accumulates and the patient's abdomen takes on the appearance of a thirty-week pregnancy.

Sometimes the symptoms completely disappear and the patient and her doctor may be convinced that there was nothing at all wrong in the first place. (I use the female pronoun because it is usually women who suffer from this disorder.) The whole incident may be blamed on an attack of food poisoning. Then the pain recurs. They are usually cramp-like, colicky pains which come and go. As the pains return the patient will notice and complain about passing sticky mucus with the faeces. The mucus comes from the mucous membranes of the colon which are fragile and filled with fine blood vessels. As the muscles of the colon tighten up and then relax the mucous membranes are easily damaged.

Doctors don't yet really know how and why the irritable colon syndrome develops. What we do know is that the wall of the colon (the lower part of the intestinal tract) is more than usually sensitive. Although it is usually women who are affected children of both sexes may develop symptoms of the syndrome. Sometimes the symptoms may mimic a grumbling appendix.

The usual symptoms (which I have already described) are pain, frequently in the left side of the abdomen, wind, sometimes building up to produce an extremely swollen and painful lower abdomen, and alternating diarrhoea and constipation. The worst attacks usually coincide with periods of extreme distress; just as patients who suffer from migraine (see p. 175) or eczema (see p. 153) have their worst symptoms when they are most severely pressured.

It is important for sufferers to realize that although their disease is a nuisance and irritating it is not dangerous, any more than migraine or eczema are dangerous. There are a number of drugs available which are said to help reduce the symptoms. Most of these drugs, however, have their drawbacks.

Treating an irritable colon basically involves treating the distressed owner of the irritated colon. Reducing the level of pressure so that it drops below the height needed to trigger off the response to the stress-threshold will almost invariably result in an amelioration of symptoms. Persistent diarrhoea in a patient with the irritable colon syndrome is an early warning sign. If no action is taken then pains and the other symptoms I have described will develop.

There are ways in which the bowel itself can be treated. Eating the right sort of foods, for example, will ensure that the colon is kept healthily busy. Modern diets are often extremely poor in fibre, the parts of edible plants that are resistant to the digestive system and which pass through virtually unchanged. Fibre provides little or nothing in the way of nourishment but it does, however, absorb water so that the contents of the digestive tract are in good shape when they leave the body. Eating fruit and vegetables in decent quantities helps solve such diverse problems as diarrhoea and constipation. It gives the colon something to get its hooped muscles around. Without fibre the faeces offer little resistance to the contracting muscles of the colon. There is no need to buy special fibre tablets although these are available. Far better and more economical to eat a good supply of fresh fruit and vegetables and to take a table-spoonful of breakfast bran as or with a morning cereal.

Learning to relax (see p. 89) is an effective way to treat colitis. One American professor of medicine who for eighteen years suffered from spells of diarrhoea, abdominal pain, wind and eructations caused by overwork and worry was cured by learning how to relax.

I should perhaps explain that the colitis I've been describing and which is also known as the irritable colon syndrome is not the same disease as the condition known as ulcerative colitis.

Ulcerative colitis is a disease which affects a relatively small number of people (about 8 in every 10,000). It usually develops in people in their twenties or thirties who are intelligent, and successful but rather modest and self-effacing. In this disorder the colon becomes actually ulcerated; it bleeds a good deal and the patient may go to his doctor complaining of the tiredness and lethargy common in severe iron deficiency anaemia. Ulcerative colitis, like the irritable colon syndrome, often disappears for months at a time and does seem to be made worse by worry. Drugs may help or surgery may be needed to remove the affected part of the bowel. It is not, however, a really dangerous illness. The important difference between this disease and the irritable colon syndrome is that in the latter bleeding is slight and unusual whereas in ulcerative colitis it is frequent and sometimes heavy.

### Constipation

When distressed some people develop diarrhoea (see p. 157), others suffer from constipation. When the constipation is brief and is accompanied by no other symptoms it can usually be relieved by nothing more powerful than a good supply of fresh fruit and bran. Oranges are particularly good for stubborn bowels. Often the disappearance of distress will be enough to solve this particular type of problem. When constipation persists a diagnosis of irritable colon syndrome should be considered.

Incidentally many people believe that they are constipated if they don't have their bowels open three times a day every day. Even when feeling off-colour and not eating properly they still feel aggrieved when denied a normal, regular motion.

In fact, of course, more than half of the general population have their bowels open normally only once a day while the number who have their bowels open three or more times a day is roughly the same as the number who have their bowels open less than once a day! The majority of the population have a bowel action between three times a week and three times a day; there are, however, quite normal people whose habits lie outside these arbitrary borders. Laxatives are often taken by people whose bowel habits are perfectly normal. For the sake of completeness it is perhaps of interest to point out that according to a paper published in the *British Journal of Clinical Practice* (November 1975) most people have their bowels open at or around breakfast time. After breakfast is the most popular moment.

Bowel disorders are caused by and cause distress in many people. An understanding of the variations accepted as normal might perhaps reduce tensions as well as the length of the queues in doctors' waiting rooms. It is important to remember that laxatives taken regularly do more harm than good.

## Cystitis

When very excited or frightened people often need to pass urine or even lose control of their bladders. Mosso and Pellacini in an article entitled 'Sur les fonctions de la vessie' showed in 1882 that bladder contractions can be influenced by feelings of mild distress. Young children and even teenage girls may get so exhilarated that they wet themselves. When nervous or agitated, as may happen just before an important interview for example, men and women notice that they need to urinate frequently; often passing small insignificant amounts of fluid each time.

The need to pass urine frequently is one of the commonest and most important symptoms of cystitis; an inflammatory disease of the bladder normally caused by an infection. It is important however to realize that frequency alone does not mean cystitis.

The patient suffering from cystitis will, in addition to complaining of a need to pass urine frequently, complain that only very small amounts are passed and invariably notices a stinging or burning sensation when the urine is passed. The urine may also be red since it is common for sufferers from cystitis to pass blood in their water. This condition is commoner in women than men for the simple anatomical reason that in women the urethra, the tube which connects the bladder to the outside world, is short. In men the urethra is longer and bugs which cause cystitis have a longer and more difficult journey to make.

There are several things that the sufferer can do to alleviate symptoms. Avoid tea, alcohol and coffee, since these substances are likely to add to the problem, but drink plenty of water or lemon squash. Since the bugs grow best in an acidic solution change your urine into an alkaline solution by drinking sodium bicarbonate or potassium citrate solution every few hours. A local pharmacist will provide you with either of these substances although in an emergency ordinary baking soda will do well.

If symptoms persist more than a day or two visit your doctor. He will possibly send off a specimen of your urine to the laboratory to find out exactly what bug you have got and he will probably prescribe an antibiotic. If he thinks he knows what the bug is he'll prescribe the antibiotic before he gets the result of the test and sometimes without doing one at all. Incidentally the symptoms of cystitis can be produced by intercourse after a long lay off or after a particularly enthusiastic love making session. This is known as honeymoon cystitis.

## Depression

I doubt if there are any readers of this book who do not know what it feels like to be depressed. Indeed, mild depression is so common and so inevitable that it cannot properly be classed as a type of illness.

Many things cause depression. Some doctors believe that depressions are often familiar; in other words that if your parents suffer from frequent bouts of depression then you will probably suffer similarly. Physical illnesses can cause depressions too. It is well known that after an attack of influenza many people feel miserable and close to tears. Virus hepatitis which is another disease caused by a virus, also makes sufferers feel extremely depressed. Anaemia diabetes (see p. 155) and many other diseases with well defined physical causes and symptoms are also known to produce symptoms of depressive illness. Women are most likely to suffer from depression just prior to a menstrual period. More than half of all accidents which involve women occur in the few days before their periods are due and over half of all female suicides occur pre-menstrually.

There is often some obvious cause for a bout of depression. The death of a close friend or relative, the approach of an anniversary or the death of a loved one, a marital break up, financial problems, legal difficulties, promotional disappointments, betrayal, frustration, failure and many other commonly experienced emotions all produce depression.

Depression is such a common result of problems such as these that, as I said a little earlier, it can hardly be described as a mental illness. It is simply a 'low' which all of us experience from time to time.

Under normal circumstances most of us recover from the shock that has produced our depression. We may still miss the friend or relative who has died but we find that the depression lifts a little with time. The fact that the job we wanted is now permanently out of reach may not be forgotten but we feel a little less depressed about it as the weeks go by. Most people can get used to anything given time.

Sometimes, of course, the depression does not lift. Months go by and still the days drag by without relief. It is then that a depression that has been caused by some specific event can be described as an illness rather than as an ordinary variation in the way we look at life.

And occasionally there is absolutely no obvious reason at all for the depression. When a depression appears quite spontaneously it is called endogenous and may be more difficult to treat.

Whatever the cause of a depression may be the symptoms which patients have do show some similarities. The depressed patient will probably be off his food and generally uninterested in the world about him. He may have difficulty in getting off to sleep at night (see p. 172) but wake up early in the morning. He may also burst into tears at the slightest provocation and be short-tempered and irritable with those close to him.

The depressed patient will usually look dejected and miserable and will only rarely take any interest in the world about him. Things that would normally have captured his closest interest will pass by without a comment. He will be slow in thinking and making decisions and more indecisive than usual. The depressed patient often begins to imagine that he is worthless and of no value to himself, his friends or his family. He may believe that he has some dreadful and incurable disease and the physical symptoms which often accompany depression (which I shall describe in a moment) may encourage that belief. He may believe that people are talking about him, plotting against him or trying to kill him.

Naturally, few patients have all these symptoms. But anyone who has more than a few for more than a day or two is probably depressed and should seek expert medical help.

The physical symptoms which I mentioned include dyspepsia or indigestion (see p. 172), constipation (see p. 147), a poor appetite and an accompanying loss of weight. These problems result from a general slowing down of the patient's bodily systems. He may also begin to sweat a good deal at night. All these symptoms, added to a feeling of lethargy and exhaustion and the weariness which follows poor sleep, simply serve to keep the depression going. It is quite common for depressed patients to believe that they have some severe physical illness.

Whatever the specific cause of depression in an individual patient it is important to remember that adversity can precipitate depression and can accentuate an existing depression. The amount of depression or distress required to depress an individual patient naturally depends largely on the personality and circumstances of the individual. Some people are better balanced and better able to cope with stress; others are more easily upset and can be depressed by minor problems. Problems can summate and a number of minor distresses can accumulate to produce a severe depression or a comparatively small problem can prove just too much for the patient who has been drifting slowly towards depression for some time.

Suicide (see p. 191) is of course an important danger with anyone suffering from depression. It should never be underestimated and I'm afraid there isn't much truth in the commonly held belief that anyone who talks about suicide won't try it. People who talk about suicide may not mean to kill themselves but if they drift into a situation where they feel they have no alternative but to try and attract help and attention by making a suicide attempt they may make a mistake and actually kill themselves. There are so many pills and poisons available these days that an accidental overdose or a slightly misjudged cry for help can easily prove fatal.

There are a number of different treatments for depression. Often, of course, the patient's friends and relatives provide support and encouragement which take him or her through the worst days. Good family relationships and a few close, reliable friends are worth more than anything the combined resources of the medical profession can offer to most depressed people. Doctors do offer support and encouragement, of course, although inevitably the time they can spend is limited unless the patient or his family can afford to pay huge bills. A small number of patients are helped by doctors listening to their problems for many weeks, months or even years and helping them sort out the sources of their discontent.

More commonly today doctors offer their depressed patients pills. During the last twenty years drug companies have produced hundreds of compounds designed to help treat depressive patients. In many cases, it is true, pharmacological help merely papers over the cracks. But there are drugs which help, sometimes by promoting sleep, sometimes by reducing the anxiety and panic which often accompanies depression and sometimes directly by helping to lift the depression. We will know a little bit more about how drugs can help depression when we know a little bit more about what happens in the brain when a patient is depressed. Meanwhile the drugs are here to stay and doctors and patients trust and believe in them for better or for worse.

Patients whose depressions do not clear with support, encouragement and pills may end up receiving electrical treatment or having a surgical operation. Electrical treatment involves giving the patient electrical shocks in an attempt to clear away the depression. This is known as electro-convulsive therapy (ECT for short). Psychosurgery for depression is of dubious value and in my book *Paper Doctors* (Temple Smith, 1977) I describe at some length why most modern doctors feel that it is an operation to be avoided at all costs (see also p. 58).

Most episodes of depression will clear up when the environmental difficulty, disordered interpersonal relationship or internal emotional conflict which caused the depression in the first place have been identified and either solved or forgotten. As always the first and most important move is to identify the cause of the depression. If this is not possible or if the depression gets worse not better as the days go by then a doctor must be consulted. Even if no immediate cure is available the doctor may be able to prevent the patient harming himself or others by arranging hospital admission.

### Dermatitis

The skin is an important vehicle for emotional expression. When frightened we turn white, when embarrassed we go red, when anxious our sweat glands work overtime. It is the skin which knows about it first when there is any confrontation between the body and its physical environment.

It is, then, hardly surprising that psychological factors are very important in worsening or prolonging skin disorders. Dermatitis or eczema (the two terms are almost interchangeable for practical purposes) as it is also known, is basically an inflammation of the cells of the skin. A large proportion of the people who suffer from this condition develop their rash after a time of difficulty or notice that when there are emotional or physical difficulties to be coped with the rash gets worse.

The skin is usually red and dry and there are small blisters to to be seen on close examination. Occasionally there will be oozing of fluid from the skin and crusts will begin to form over the worst areas of dermatitis.

Young children and even babies often develop dermatitis.

Sometimes there will be a family history of a stress-threshold illness: One or other parent will have had migraine (see p. 175), asthma (see p. 135), hay fever (see p. 123) or eczema. When it starts in young children dermatitis often appears first on the face and scalp although it may also affect the rest of the body. It always itches a great deal and the persistent scratching sometimes produces sores and infections.

After the age of two the eczema usually gets a little better by itself although in some children it may seem to get worse on the backs of the knees and in the bends of the elbows.

Although many children with eczema do develop asthma not all children have both problems and mothers should certainly not sit waiting for asthma to develop. Ironically, if asthma does develop then the skin condition usually clears up when the asthma is at its worst. There is no way to tell whether or not an infantile eczema will last for life or will improve as time goes by. I believe that mothers should be as optimistic as they can be since pessimism will not only make the skin condition worse but it will also make the child less able to live with the problem should it persist.

Many cases of eczema or dermatitis are caused in the first instance by contact with foreign substances. Some people develop skin reactions when they come into contact with certain types of metal. Some women and transvestites, for example, develop skin rashes when they wear brassieres with nickel buckles or clips and some men develop similar reactions to the metal of their watch straps. Occasionally women develop rashes as a result of wearing jewellery. Some powders and creams can be responsible for skin rashes. Deodorants, dyes, bleaches, and soaps are often identified as having caused rashes. At Christmas time every year doctors see dozens of patients who have allergies to new Christmas presents. Once a patient has been identified as being allergic to a specific substance the only real solution is to keep them away from it. Cotton lined rubber gloves may prove an adequate barrier for men or women coming into contact with oils or detergents at work or home but usually the only solution is to keep the patient and the responsible chemical apart.

154

Whether an eczema has developed from birth, been brought on by contact with something or has simply developed in later years the treatment is much the same. In the short term hydrocortisone creams or ointments are the answer. Only available on a doctor's prescription these creams can clear up a rash in ten days or a fortnight but, if the factor which originally caused the rash is not dealt with, the rash will return quickly and will probably be difficult to deal with next time. Hydrocortisone creams should not be used for long periods since they can produce skin problems themselves. Because these creams and ointments are powerful they should only be used for rashes which have been seen by a doctor. It is dangerous to use them for the treatment of other minor skin conditions. Very often when one cream which has been useful for some months proves ineffective a change to another variety of cream may provide a semi-miraculous (though perhaps temporary) result.

Whatever the initiating factor responsible for the development of dermatitis there is little doubt that distress can make a bad skin condition worse and produce a flare up of a dormant skin trouble.

## Diabetes

There are said to be 50 million diabetics in the world. In most western countries about three per cent of the adult population is diabetic and there are probably as many undiagnosed diabetics as there are known diabetics.

Diabetes is caused by a breakdown of the normal mechanism by which the body uses up sugar. We don't really know why the mechanism breaks down but we do know that obesity and advancing years sometimes precipitate the development of diabetes. There is often a family history of the disease in younger diabetics.

When a non-diabetic eats carbohydrates such as bread, potatoes and cakes the glucose that is produced from the breakdown of the carbohydrate is absorbed into the blood stream. The glucose provides energy and is used by the tissues to help rebuild and restore damaged and worn out tissue. For the sugar in the blood to be used properly a substance called insulin is needed; this is made in the pancreas and automatically pumped into the blood when required.

In a diabetic the glucose is produced from carbohydrates in the normal way but there is no insulin available. Without insulin the level of sugar in the blood rises; eventually sugar will become so plentiful in the blood that it starts to be passed in the urine in an attempt to get rid of it. The patient without enough insulin will normally complain of feeling tired, and thirsty, losing weight and passing great quantities of urine. If these early symptoms of diabetes go unnoticed the patient may become unconscious.

There is no cure for diabetes but the disease can be effectively controlled in several ways. Sometimes, particularly when the newly discovered diabetic is elderly, controlling the amount of carbohydrate eaten will be all that is necessary. Occasionally tablets may help by stimulating the production of insulin in the body. Most frequently in younger diabetics insulin injections will be needed. The patient simply injects insulin into his or her body at regular intervals. It is, of course, essential that if tablets or insulin injections are being used the diet should be carefully controlled.

These controlling methods are so effective that most of the people with diabetes live perfectly normal lives. Many are successful sportsmen since the only important criterion is that the intake of insulin and carbohydrate must be carefully calculated to match the projected energy expenditure.

When a known diabetic begins to lose consciousness there are two possible explanations. Firstly it is possible that the amount of insulin put into the body has not been enough to cope with the amount of sugar; secondly it is possible that the amount of insulin has been too great. Differentiating between the symptoms of these two explanations is not easy but it is generally reasonable for anyone finding a known diabetic semiconscious to give sugar by mouth. A couple of sugar lumps or a very sweet drink will do the job. If the blood sugar is too low because of an excessive insulin dose the sugar given by mouth will probably bring the patient round. If the blood sugar is already high the additional small quantity taken by mouth will make very little difference.

It is important that all diabetics learn as much as they can about their illness. A clear understanding of the possible complications and the various potential hazards will usually help the patient a great deal. It always helps of course if the patient's friends and relatives are also aware of the problems facing the diabetic and how best they can help.

The first society organized to help patients with a specific disease was created at the suggestion of H. G. Wells, himself a diabetic, in 1934. Today the Diabetic Association in Britain has sister societies throughout the world. These societies produce a great deal of helpful literature and provide diabetics with the opportunities to give and receive help and advice.

Although diabetes is not produced or caused by distress it is one of the diseases which can be made worse by pressure. Apart from the practical problems of eating properly and carefully calculated meals when under pressure there is the fact that patients who are suffering emotional problems or who are inhibiting the outward manifestations of emotion will develop an increase in the level of their blood sugar. The first evidence of this was produced by R. Boehm and F. A. Hoffman in 1878 and their results were confirmed by Bulatao in the *American Journal of Physiology* in 1925.

It is therefore likely that diabetics may find their control being disrupted by distress while non-diabetics may exhibit the signs and symptoms of diabetes for the first time when under pressure. Anyone who has the symptoms I have described should have a sample of urine checked and anyone with a family history of diabetes should have a urine sample checked by their doctor every year or two. If you don't like to ask your doctor ask a diabetic friend or relative to do the test for you.

### Diarrhoea
Diarrhoea (the passing of liquid faeces frequently) is a common symptom of distress. It is, for example, a problem often suffered by soldiers before a battle, students before an examination and sportsmen before an event. When the diarrhoea is short-lasting and self-limiting, treatment may be unnecessary. If particularly inconvenient the diarrhoea may perhaps be controlled by a bottle of kaolin purchased from the chemist or a

supply of codeine tablets prescribed by a doctor. When the diarrhoea persists, however, a diagnosis of irritable colon syndrome (see p. 144) may be appropriate. Diarrhoea that lasts more than two or three days is worth reporting to your doctor.

**Eczema**
See under dermatitis (see p. 153).

**Epilepsy**
Epilepsy is a symptom not a disease. The brain, like the computer, depends for its functioning on electrical activity. Occasionally, because of damage to brain cells or some inherited abnormality there is a short circuit. When this happens in a computer there will be a malfunction; when it happens in the human brain strange events may occur. We call these events fits. A minor fit, caused by a small electrical problem, may go unnoticed and involve nothing more than a momentary lapse of attention. A major fit will be easily recognized. The sufferer will fall to the ground and jerk violently. Frothing at the mouth, incontinence and unconsciousness are common accompaniments.

One in every two hundred people has epilepsy and most are well controlled. Although some jobs (flying aeroplanes or working as steeplejacks) are not suitable, epileptics can do most jobs with the usual training. Driving is no problem when the epilepsy has been controlled and a perfectly normal family life is the rule rather than the exception. Between fits the epileptic's brain functions quite normally.

People who suffer from epilepsy usually know that fits are likely to be triggered by a number of different stimuli. Alcohol, inadequate meals, distress, insufficient sleep and rest and flickering lights (such as the ones which happen when the television set goes wrong) can trigger a fit in susceptible people. Sufferers often have some warning before an attack, feeling uneasy and irritable for some time before, and having an aura or special warning just before the attack. The aura varies from person to person and may involve a special sensation such as nausea or a flashback during which past events seem quite clear. The aura

158

may give sufficient warning to enable the patient to lie down and keep away from any dangerous machinery.

Fits are sometimes a sign that the pressure under which a patient is working or the problems which have accumulated at home are too much for him to cope with satisfactorily. In other words when an epileptic has a fit, if there are no other obvious triggers, the fit may be a warning sign that the body has reached its stress threshold. Obviously when this is the case the solution is to reduce the pressure of living and to ease off a little.

Most epileptics will need to take regular medication to help damp down and prevent fits. Phenobarbitone is still one of the most widely prescribed drugs for the control of epilepsy although there are, of course, many dozens of other drugs available. People who are subject to fits can not only avoid fits by steering clear of trigger factors as often as possible but can also protect themselves against damage caused during a fit by a little careful thought. It is obviously wise for an epileptic to carry identification, such as a Medic Alert necklace or bracelet, to warn and inform strangers in an emergency. Without such identification an epileptic may be mistaken for a drunk. It is also wise for epileptics to use guards over open fires, to avoid buying sharp pointed furniture and to use as little water as possible in the bath to avoid drowning.

If a fit does occur it is clearly helpful if people likely to be around know what to do. They shouldn't try to move the fitting patient but should put something soft under his head and turn the head to one side. Ties and clothing around the neck should be loosened. If possible a folded handkerchief or some other piece of soft material should be placed between the teeth to prevent damage inside the mouth. If the teeth are already tightly clenched don't try forcing anything through them. Bitten tongues heal, broken teeth don't.

It is important not to try and restrain the epileptic's movements nor to try to feed drink or tablets through the clenched teeth. There is no need at all to call a doctor unless one fit is followed immediately by another fit without the patient regaining consciousness.

159

**Headache**

The commonest cause of a headache is tension. The man who has had a busy day at work, been stuck in a traffic jam for two hours and been worrying about a business deal will probably develop one. The woman who has been battling her way through crowded stores, who has missed her bus and been hurrying to get home before the children get in from school may have one. Tension headaches are a common sign that the stress threshold has been reached.

Tension headaches are caused by a sustained, painful contraction of the muscles around the face, scalp and neck. The headache, which usually seems throbbing and may affect any part of the head, will invariably disappear if the patient sits quietly for a while and perhaps takes a couple of mild analgesic tablets.

When under pressure, worried or particularly determined we often grit out teeth and frown in concentration. Look at yourself in the mirror next time you're concentrating and you'll be surprised at the furrows in your brow! If you stop and think for a moment when next sitting in a traffic jam you will probably discover that you can actually feel the tension in your neck and face muscles.

There are, of course, many other causes of headache. Headaches across the forehead, accompanied by a feeling of stuffiness and a difficulty in breathing are often caused by sinusitis and catarrh. They may be worse in the morning and are sometimes helped by a warm shower. These may need antibiotic tablets before they clear up. An infected tooth can cause a headache which seems to spread far beyond the area of tissue around the tooth. Indeed, sometimes the pain seems to be completely unrelated to the tooth itself. The pain is transmitted by nerves which pass nearby the tooth. Toothache may merit a visit to the dentist but if an infection is causing the problem you will probably have to take antibiotic before the tooth can be dealt with.

High blood pressure (see p. 167) may cause headaches which are worse on waking and which are concentrated at the back of the head. People who, because of poor lighting conditions or poor eyesight, squint a great deal when reading or studying figures may develop headaches which are worse in the evenings and are concentrated at the front of the head. These headaches are caused by screwing up the muscles around the eyes. Ear infections cause headaches, usually around the ears.

Alcohol, of course, is also a cause of headaches. To avoid an alcohol-induced headache and the other accompanying feelings of being hung over drink plenty of water after a heavy consumption of alcohol.

Arthritis (see p. 185) in the cervical spine, the neck, is another common cause of headache. Less common causes include an inflammatory disease known as temporal arteritis and the various types of brain tumour which are all rare. Meningitis, an uncommon inflammation of the covering over the brain, also causes headache and neck stiffness. Migraine, a common cause of headache is discussed elsewhere (see p. 175). It usually causes a one-sided headache which is accompanied by a feeling of nausea or actual sickness. And of course bumps and bangs on the head cause pain!

But the commonest cause of a headache is worry. Paradoxically the pains are usually at their worst when the problems which caused the worry have ceased. Experts believe that this is because during relaxation the blood flow into the brain changes. In times of tension there is an increased flow of blood into the brain caused probably by the tensing of muscles, when the muscles relax the blood flow decreases. Most worry headaches can be treated at home with soluble aspirin or paracetamol tablets and plenty of rest. But if a headache lasts more than a day, is accompanied by vomiting or follows a blow on the head then call the doctor.

### Heart attacks (see also angina pectoris p. 126)

Every year in Europe more than a million men and women die of heart trouble. A similar number die in America. In Britain alone 60,000 men and women under the age of sixty-five die suddenly and often unexpectedly of heart disease. Men aged between forty-five and fifty-five are most at risk. Although a number of those deaths are caused by heart failure, itself triggered by faulty valves or worn out muscles, most of the younger

161

people who die of heart disease have healthy hearts. They die because the arteries which supply their heart muscles with blood become clogged and unable to carry fresh supplies of food and oxygen.

About the size of its owner's fist, the human heart pumps between 10 and 50 pints of blood every minute, depending upon the body's needs. To do this the average heart must beat 70 times a minute, 100,000 times a day, 36 million times a year and about 2,500 million times in an average lifetime. Inevitably, any piece of machinery which has a workload like that needs some looking after. The coronary arteries which encircle the heart provide the raw materials which enable the heart to operate and take away the waste products which might otherwise accumulate and cause damage.

There are a number of factors which affect the ability of the coronary arteries to function efficiently and effectively. Researchers have shown that people who drink soft water are more at risk of developing coronary artery disease than are people who drink hard water, that people who exercise, such as bus conductors, are less at risk than people who don't, such as bus drivers, and that high blood pressure (see p. 167), excess weight and eating animal fats increase the likelihood of a heart attack (see p. 80).

Heart attacks can be caused by a sudden exposure to cold weather, by a sudden fright or a great surge of excitement. A number of people die every year while watching television programmes. Sporting events, such as football matches, are particularly likely to cause heart attacks in excited viewers. Smoking damages the coronary arteries since one of the substances in tobacco makes blood vessels contract. In Finland about 3,500 working age men die each year from heart attacks (also known as coronaries, and myocardial infarctions) and of these approximately 3,300 are smokers. The majority of men who die from heart attacks are cigarette smokers although there are of course exceptions to the rule. (For advice on smoking control see p. 88.) People who are overweight are also liable to develop coronary artery disease. (For advice on weight control see p. 65.) A thin muscular lively child is far less less likely to develop heart disease in later life than a chubby sedentary child.

Another important cause of heart attacks is mental strain. Soviet doctors have confirmed many times that there is a strong link between coronary artery disease and exposure to noise and vibrations or pressure at work. The surgeon John Hunter remarked 300 years ago that his life would be at the mercy of anyone who made him angry. Mr Hunter died during a board meeting at his hospital. Friedman and Rosenman, two American researchers who have specialized in studying the effects of strain on the heart, studied a group of accountants. They found that when the April tax deadline approached the accountants were more likely to have heart attacks. At other times of the year, when their other habits remained the same, they were safer. Dr Malcolm Carruthers, a London pathologist, believes that strain and pressure leads to a reaction which narrows coronary arteries and makes blood clots more likely. Both the narrowing and the development of clots are, of course, factors which impede the flow of blood into the heart muscles.

In 1910 William Osler suggested that severe emotional strain could contribute to coronary artery disease. The same argument has been put forward many times since then. It has, of course, always been difficult to decide exactly what comprises emotional strain. A doctor in Birmingham, England, did point out in 1954 that the life of a physician in a big city must be less stressful than that of a peasant in the Yangtse valley concerned with flood, famine, pestilence and war. In theory that may be right but the big city physician may well worry more about his taxes, his children's education and his career, than the Yangtse peasant worries about the risk of flood or pestilence. The city doctor thinks he ought to be able to cope with his problems. The Yangtse peasant knows he has no chance of dealing with flood or pestilence.

George L. Engel of the University of Rochester School of Medicine in New York State reported that a fifty-five year old doctor had a heart attack when passed over for promotion. Pope Innocent IV and King Philip V are both said to have died of anguish after their armies had lost battles. Many doctors believe that the strain of being in an intensive care unit or coronary care unit may be enough to cause a heart attack. In one study eighty per cent of the patients in one of these special units were worried by all the machinery there and showed symptoms of anxiety. Anxiety (see p. 131), of course, is one of the things that can trigger off a heart attack!

Ambitious, competitive people are said to be at risk as are those who move house a lot, change their work a great deal or move from one part of the country to another. All these factors lead to an increase in pressure and a decrease in stability. People who work hard, who get irritable easily and who worry a great deal are all more likely to have heart attacks than more phlegmatic, peaceful characters. Worrying about an illness (particularly an increased likelihood of developing a heart condition) can produce a heart attack. Paradoxically, of course, some people who worry about themselves look after their own health so well that they survive much longer than all their relatives or peers.

Whatever its cause, and inevitably when a man has a heart attack there will probably be a number of possible causes, the symptoms of a coronary are very clear. Patients usually complain of a tight, constricting pain in the chest. They are usually short of breath, pale and sweating. The pain can cause sickness. Very often the pain is not confined to the chest but goes up into the jaw and down the arms. The left is more common than the right. It is invariably quite clear that they are ill.

When a man or woman has a heart attack the first things to do are to sit down and keep them warm. Exercise and cold can both make the symptoms worse. Call for medical help straight away. If a doctor comes he'll probably bring an ampule of morphine or heroin which can be injected straight into a vein or into muscles. This will provide almost instant relief. If there isn't any chance of finding a doctor but powerful painkillers are available they can be given by mouth. Ordinary pain killer such as aspirin or paracetomol will do little to relieve the pain of a coronary attack.

Doctors used to believe that all patients who had heart attacks should be looked after in hospital. A few years ago hospitals were busily building and equipping special coronary care units where patients who had had heart attacks could be looked after. Today doctors aren't quite so sure. A patient who has just had a heart attack will inevitably be worried and weak. A journey to the hospital may kill him. No less than sixty per cent of the patients with heart attacks who are moved die before they even reach hospital. Once there the chances of the doctors in the special unit being able to do anything to prevent a second attack are slim. Statisticians claim that the effectiveness of coronary care units is so slight that it is difficult to measure their usefulness. The alternative of course is to keep the patient at home. A number of studies have shown that if the patient can be kept warm and quiet at home he will have a better chance of making a good recovery.

A number of patients will not make good recoveries, of course, whether they are kept at home or sent to hospital. Those patients whose heart muscle is severely damaged or whose coronary arteries are badly damaged and diseased may need to have surgery. Today's cardiac surgeons do not just do heart transplant operations. They do some operations to clear out congested coronary arteries or to replace them with new arteries. These new arteries are often made from the patient's own veins, taken usually from the legs!

The majority of patients who have had heart attacks do recover and can look forward to a normal life. Neither they nor their relatives need worry about needing to take special care although changes must usually be made. When work can be resumed depends naturally enough upon the type of work. A man whose job involves lifting bricks and timber on a building site will need to have a longer convalescence than a man whose job involves no heavy mental or physical work. The precise length of convalescence depends very much upon the individual's progress.

During the early post attack months it is important to avoid physical exertion and to keep away from situations likely to produce pressure. Heavy exercise and emotional strain both put heavy demands upon the heart and anger, fear and worry and too much responsibility too soon, are all as dangerous as heavy labouring work.

The patient should start exercising slowly, and gradually build up the amount he does. Golf is a perfect game for the convalescent heart attack victim as long as he doesn't get too involved in competitive sport. As soon as any pain starts all exercise should be stopped for a few minutes. Warning anginal pains (see p. 126) should be treated with the special pills that are invariably prescribed.

Whatever the weather, heart attack victims should try to keep themselves at a fairly steady temperature. When it is cold they should do less exercise than usual in an attempt to reduce the strain upon the heart. Tobacco is totally taboo and any excess weight should be shed as soon as possible. Heavy meals should be avoided by all and a rest for twenty minutes or so after a meal will help give the body time to cope with exercise. Many doctors believe that animal fats (such as those in butter) are bad for the heart.

Patients who have had heart attacks often refrain from sexual intercourse for many months in the mistaken belief that they are likely to trigger off another attack if they risk such exercise. This can be a mistake. Both partners may suffer frustrations and one may worry that the other might be tempted to seek comfort elsewhere. There are of course many ways of love making which do not leave the participants exhausted and dripping with perspiration. When a heart attack victim is beginning to resume normal activities in the bedroom it might be wise for his partner to take a more active role. The male heart attack victim should lie flat on his back and allow his consort to take the initiative. Intercourse can easily be completed enjoyably with the female partner kneeling astride her man.

The patient who has had a heart attack, and indeed the patient who fears that he might have a heart attack, will naturally enough want to know how best to avoid this most frightening condition. The two most important things are to lose excess weight and to give up smoking. Few men should weigh more than fourteen stone. As a very rough guide knock off about a stone from this for every two inches you are below six feet and you'll get your ideal fighting weight.

Giving up smoking is easy. Mark Twain said it was so easy that he'd done it hundreds of times. In another part of this book I describe some methods which might help readers give up smoking (see p. 88). Exercise is another important aid for the man who wants to avoid a heart attack (see p. 84). Learning to relax is another way that a potential heart attack victim can protect himself (see p. 89). Finally, any man or woman who has had an attack of angina should regard this as an early warning. Avoiding a heart attack is much more fun than recovering from one.

The table that follows shows occupational influences on deaths caused by coronary artery disease. A standardized mortality ratio of 100 would be an average for all workers. (Figures from the Registrar General's Occupational Mortality tables.)

| | | |
|---|---|---|
| Company directors | 758 | |
| Coalmine face workers | 231 | |
| Unskilled workers (general) | 172 | |
| Ships' officers, pilots | 152 | |
| Dockers | 151 | above average |
| Civil Servants | 118 | |
| Doctors | 118 | |
| Shop assistants | 101 | |
| Carpenters | 101 | |

| | | |
|---|---|---|
| Telephone operators | 97 | |
| MPs, senior govt. officers | 97 | |
| Accountants | 93 | |
| Clergy | 90 | |
| Electricians | 83 | below average |
| Gardeners, groundsmen | 82 | |
| Foresters, woodsmen | 77 | |
| Teachers | 60 | |
| Authors | 53 | |
| Secretaries and typists | 36 | |

**Hypertension**

A third of the entire American adult population is said to suffer from hypertension (high blood pressure). Strokes (see p. 189) and heart attacks (see p. 161), two diseases commonly caused by high blood pressure, occur at earlier and earlier ages. Today both these disorders are common among men in their thirties and by no means unknown among men in their twenties. Three factors are thought to be responsible: bad eating habits, a lack of exercise and an increase in the pressure of living. These causes are all interlinked.

High blood pressure is commonest amongst people whose occupations expose them to frequent mental strains, excess responsibilities and conflicting situations. Teachers and bank clerks, for example, are more likely to develop high blood pressure than farmers or gardeners. Engine drivers, telephone operators, taxidrivers and casualty surgeons are more likely to have high blood pressure than accountants, dermatologists or clergymen. People who find it difficult to adapt to new situations are at particular risk because they suffer for longer when in difficult situations. They are likely to brood over their diffi- ties. Self-employed people building up businesses and working long hours suffer because of the number of problems and the inability to escape from them. Those who are basically aggressive and hostile but whose jobs do not allow them to assert themselves are at particular risk. One man with high blood pressure who gave in once to temptation and physically attacked an opponent had a much lower blood pressure immediately after the attack.

Hypertension affects the heart, the blood vessels and the kidneys even though in the early stages it produces no specific symptoms of its own. Although we know little about what causes high blood pressure in most people we do know that narrowing of the arteries through the body can result in the development of high blood pressure. To travel around the body blood has to be subjected to pressure; the same way as we get water round the plumbing of a house. It is the beating heart which keeps the blood under pressure and if the arteries through which the blood is flowing are narrowed the blood travels with more force just as when you squeeze a garden hose pipe the water shoots out faster and further. In a disease called atherosclerosis or arteriosclerosis the walls of the arteries become thicker and less pliant. The hole inside the arteries becomes narrower. Naturally it is more difficult to push blood along these narrowed arteries at the rate necessary to keep the supply of blood to the tissues at the previous rate. The pressure goes up, the thinner stream of blood travels faster and the heart muscles enlarge with the extra work, just as the weightlifters' biceps get bigger when he practises lifting his weights.

The enlarged heart will itself need more blood to supply its enlarged muscles but the coronary arteries cannot enlarge and may have themselves developed atherosclerosis. The heart muscles will therefore be deprived of oxygen. Angina (see p. 126) and possibly a heart attack (see p. 161) may result. The high blood pressure in narrow arteries is likely to burst finer capillary vessels. If this happens in the brain the patient is said to have had a stroke (see p. 189). The narrowed arteries are easily blocked by clots. Again strokes may result.

Atherosclerotic arteries also develop in the kidneys. These narrowed arteries reduce the flow of blood into the kidneys which have a self-protecting system which releases a hormone designed to *increase* the blood pressure. The general rise in blood pressure which results further damages the arteries in the kidney (by pushing more cholesterol into the artery walls) and so the supply of blood is worse than ever. The hormone is released in larger quantities and eventually the kidneys simply fail.

The machine used to measure blood pressure is called a sphygmomanometer. When the medical examiner wraps the cuff of the machine around the upper part of the patient's arm he connects the cuff to a rubber tube leading to a column of mercury. The cuff, which is usually made of cloth, contains a rubber bag which is inflated by squeezing on a rubber bulb. When the pressure inside the cuff has been built up to equal the pressure of the blood in the arteries of the arm the blood is stopped. So if the doctor feels for a pulse at the wrist he won't feel anything. Nor will he hear anything through his stethoscope when he tries to listen to the flow of blood at the inside of the elbow. The column of the mercury simply measures the air pressure inside the rubber bag in the cloth cuff. When the pressure in the cuff is lowered the blood starts to flow through the arteries again.

If the column of mercury is measured at 120 millimetres when the flow of blood is stopped then the systolic blood pressure (the pressure exerted on the blood when the heart is actually beating) is said to be 120 millimetres of mercury. If the column of mercury is measured at 80 millimetres of mercury when the blood is simply travelling through the artery and waiting for the next boost from the heart then the diastolic measurement is said to be 80 millimetres of mercury.

A normal blood pressure in a young, healthy adult is about 120 over 80 but age, sex and general health all affect individual blood pressures. A seventy year old healthy man will probably have a blood pressure of 150 over 100.

Although blood pressure may rise and remain high for several years before any symptoms appear there are signs which suggest a rise in blood pressure. The most important is the development of headaches at the back of the head which are worst on getting up in the morning. However, anyone who is under pressure at work or at home, or who has other signs of physical distress, should have a blood pressure check up, and anyone who has high blood pressure should have regular checks and ensure that if treatment is prescribed it is maintained. There is no permanent pharmacological cure for high blood pressure.

When a case of hypertension has been diagnosed the doctor will probably begin treatment by giving the patient a drug to help relax him a little since many hypertensive patients are living under stress. A relaxant drug will often bring the blood pressure down. Doctors also use a wide variety of drugs called diuretics. These drugs bring down the blood pressure by making the kidneys work a little harder at expelling unwanted fluids from the body. If you reduce the amount of fluid in the body the blood pressure inevitably falls. More specific therapies are kept for those patients who do not respond to these other drugs.

Incidentally, some patients who are on drugs for high blood pressure become dizzy occasionally. This happens when the blood pressure is lowered too much. The dizziness will usually occur when the patient stands up or gets out of bed. To avoid this problem patients taking blood pressure drugs should move their position with some care.

Most promisingly it has been shown that by learning to relax properly people with hypertension can bring their blood pressure down. An articles in the *Journal of Chronic Diseases* in 1974 written by a team led by Dr Herbert Benson of the Beth Israel Hospital in Boston, Massachusetts showed that meditation is an effective method of lowering high blood pressure. Dr Benson points out that relaxation is easily learned, inexpensive and has no side effects (see p. 89).

## Impotence

A single isolated instance of impotence may seem like the end of the world to a previously successful and virile male. And yet there is often a simple and reassuring explanation for the failing. Most instances of impotence result from anxiety (see p. 131). Overwork (see p. 179) is a common cause of impotence. The man who is struggling hard at the office is not in the best physical condition for love-making. Impotence has been described as the Houseman's Disease since young hospital doctors work such long and tiring hours that they are sometimes unable to take advantage of any extra facilities made available in the nurses' home.

When impotence occurs without other physical symptoms such as pain or difficulty in passing urine it can usually be accepted as having a psychological origin.

Erections and ejaculations involve reflexes which may not be under direct voluntary control but factors such as tiredness do affect the efficiency of those reflexes. Alcohol is another factor which has an influence on potency. Too much of it may increase the desire but at the same time dash any hope of converting the desire into an accomplishment.

Any man who experiences impotence should rest assured that his manhood is unlikely to have been lost without just cause. The best way to treat the disorder is to enlist the help of the disappointed partner. Sympathy, support and gentle encouragement, allied with prolonged rest, reduction in work commitments and a mild tranquillizer (a glass of whisky perhaps) should solve the problem. Early morning experiments are likely to be most successful.

Worrying about failure can, of course, start off a cycle of

depression (see p. 149) and anxiety (see p. 131) which results in the impotence being prolonged. The longer it goes on the worse it gets.

## Indigestion

Indigestion (also known as dyspepsia) is usually confined to the centre of the chest and invariably occurs a short while after eating. It may occur when food is eaten too quickly and may be a sign of nothing more threatening than the over hasty consumption of an unusually spicy or fatty meal.

Indigestion sufferers who find that they cannot control their symptoms by swallowing antacids or who have regular attacks of pain occurring after fairly small and ordinarily digestible meals should visit their doctor. Any local pharmacist will be able to recommend an antacid and will probably be delighted to offer you a bottle of his own special brand of mixture. This is likely to be cheaper than a proprietary mixture and just as good since it will undoubtedly contain much the same in the way of ingredients. Sodium bicarbonate is a good emergency solution to an attack of indigestion and even a glass of milk may help. On page 79 there are a number of dietary rules which should help sufferers avoid further attacks of pain.

It is important to remember that regular attacks of indigestion merit a visit to your doctor. It is particularly important to follow this advice if you have also lost weight.

## Insomnia

The quantity and quality of sleep we get is very important for it is during sleep that our batteries recharge and our brain sorts itself out. During the daytime, millions of pieces of information are fed into the average human brain, and after sixteen or seventeen hours it is beginning to feel slightly information-logged. It needs a rest.

Just as different brains do different things with the same information, so different brains need varying amounts of time in which to recover from the input of all this information. The amount of sleep needed varies just about as much as finger-prints vary. A newborn baby may need fifteen hours a day, and while one adult may get by with six hours every twenty-four hour period, another may feel tired and irritable without nine hours sleep. The average is about eight hours a night. If a man who needs eight hours of sleep a night has only seven, then he will wake up bad-tempered and apparently slow-wittted the next day. He will not catch up until he gets to sleep again. If we spend several nights without sleep, then we may need twelve or fifteen hours sleep to recover.

There are many ways to improve the quality and quantity of your sleep. Firstly, you must make sure you are tired when you go to bed. And you need to be physically tired, not just mentally exhausted. If you try to go to bed after working on books and paperwork for hours, then you will probably find the problems you have been thinking about insist on reappearing in your brain at regular intervals. Go for a walk before you go to bed. If it is pouring with rain, or you have just washed your hair, do a few exercises and then relax in front of the television set or with a good book. Don't read a heavy academic book while trying to prepare for sleep. Read a light detective novel or a romantic story.

Your bed must be comfortable if you are going to sleep well. Good beds are not cheap, but you will probably spend a third of your life in bed, so don't cut corners too much! You will need to be warm as well if you are going to sleep properly. If you can't stand the weight of enough blankets, then what about hot water bottles, electric blankets and such old-fashioned ideas as bed socks? Stuffy bedrooms are difficult to sleep in, so make sure there is plenty of ventilation. Cigarette smoking may keep many people awake, so don't let smokers come upstairs with their cigarettes.

There are many things which can keep you awake. Pain, of course, will prevent sleep. Many muscular aches and pains seem worse at night than during the daytime. See your doctor if a couple of soluble aspirins or paracetomol tablets do not ease off aching in your limbs. Hunger can also keep you awake. Try a milky drink and a couple of biscuits at night, but avoid big heavy meals full of spices and 'hot' foods. If you live in a noisy house, ear plugs may help, and double glazing may also cut down on the amount of noise from outside.

Depression (see p. 149) or anxiety (see p. 131) can also keep people awake, and here the treatment may include pills, but although sleeping pills may solve the problem of sleeplessness, antidepressant pills are much more likely to solve the problem in the long term. For these you will have to visit the doctor. Explain your problems; don't just ask for sleeping pills! Dealing with the cause of anxiety or depression will provide an even more effective and permanent solution.

The two best remedies for sleeplessness are alcohol and sex in moderate quantities.

### Menstrual disorders

Many women notice that in the few days prior to a menstrual period they feel low both physically and mentally. Specifically they may complain of headaches, swollen ankles, tender, swollen breasts and of depression and irritability. Changes in hormone levels within the body are believed to be responsible. There is plenty of evidence which shows that women are less successful in tests requiring mental or physical endeavour during the week before a period starts and there is also evidence suggesting that crises inspired by behavioural disorders are more likely to occur in the premenstrual week.

Most women will confirm that the hormonal changes associated with the menstrual cycle result in an increased susceptibility to anxiety and distress at particular times of the month. In particular, the days before a period are often associated with a high level of tension and a tendency towards irritability and impatience. It is unlikely that outside strains or pressures have any appreciable influence on the physiological changes associated with the menstrual cycle but those changes do have a very appreciable influence on a woman's ability to cope with and deal with provocative or worrying situations.

Emotional women and women who are under other outside strains and pressures are, of course, more likely to suffer from premenstrual tension. The hormonal strains produced before a period added to the other pressures which exist mean that the woman is more likely to exhibit signs of being under pressure. A woman who feels irritable before a period may be able to control her feelings if she doesn't have personal or environmental problems to cope with. When under environmental or personal strain she may react more violently than usual.

The contraceptive pill, which controls the physiological changes associated with the menstrual cycle also has an effect on the taker's mental state. Some women find that it makes them more able to cope with external pressures, others find that the opposite happens.

In her forties or fifties, when she reaches the menopause, a woman has a different problem to cope with. There is a fall in the quantity of female hormones circulating in the body and without these the monthly periods stop. The actual lack of hormones may cause some physical problems. For example, the vagina sometimes becomes dry and painful. But many of the ensuing problems are psychological. The lack of regular periods is worrying to many women who accept the change as a definite sign of their declining years and fading femininity. Others, more practical, welcome the opportunity it gives to enjoy sex without fear of pregnancy.

There is undoubtedly a strong interaction between anxiety (see p. 131) and the problems commonly associated with the menopause. Worry and strains exacerbate the natural fears of a woman who is probably also seeing her own children grow up and leave home and having to re-establish her own role in life. Hormonal replacements are commonly used these days to help alleviate the physical symptoms associated with the menopause and there is little doubt that these supplementary hormones also help alleviate the psychological problems.

## Migraine

Migraines are a type of headache but the causes, symptoms and treatments are so special, affect so many people and are so related to distress and pressure that the disorder merits a section of its own. Migraine is frequently a warning that the stress threshold has been reached.

Millions of working days are lost each year through migraine. The sufferers are said to have included Lewis Carroll, Darwin, Freud, Joan of Arc, Rudyard Kipling, Nietzsche and Jefferson. It has been said that ten per cent of the population (women more than men) have migraine attacks from time to time. The symptoms vary a great deal but usually include some gastro-intestinal signs in addition to a searing headache. Nausea and vomiting or one of these symptoms alone is the usual accompaniment. Before the headache there is usually a warning aura. Some sufferers see flaring lights. Visual disturbances are common. Migraines usually begin in the sufferer's teens and may persist throughout the victim's life. They occur at irregular intervals, sometimes once or twice a week, usually less frequently.

The cause of migraine is still something of a mystery but it seems likely that the blood vessels supplying the brain constrict and then dilate, reducing and then increasing the flow of blood to the brain. The initial constriction causes the aura, the following dilation produces the pain. In tension headache the pain is caused by too much blood flowing into the brain. The same thing happens in high blood pressure. In migraine it is often the blood vessels on one side of the head that are affected; hence the result that the headache occurs on one side of the head.

Migraine attacks are triggered off by many different things. Sometimes a specific factor can be found which causes the attacks. Chocolate, cheese, oranges, lemons, shell fish, alcohol, bananas and fried foods have been described as causing migraine attacks. A friend of mine had frequent migraine attacks until he gave up smoking cigars. To find out whether or not any of these triggers is responsible a migraine sufferer must keep a close record of all his or her activities for a month or two. Only then may a pattern showing some relationship between migraine attacks and a foodstuff be discovered. Making lists may be tiresome but it does frequently help pinpoint a cause.

When migraine attacks are caused by distress they usually occur when the subject is relaxing. Migraine attacks often occur at weekends. Any form of excitement may produce the telltale symptom of a migraine attack. Pleasure as well as unhappiness can produce the pain.

When an attack occurs the pain and discomfort may be relieved to some extent by ordinary pain killers but often something more powerful is needed. The classical treatment is the drug called ergotamine tartrate which helps by constricting the dilated arteries supplying the brain. The ergotamine does not, however, help relieve the visual symptoms. Other drugs are said to help by reducing the responsiveness of cranial arteries and slowing down their ability to respond to stimuli triggering their enlargement or constriction. Many researchers have shown that various forms of relaxation (see p. 89) are the best way of preventing and dealing with migraine attacks.

## Nightmares

Although children commonly have nightmares adults suffer from them less frequently. When they occur and recur there is usually a psychological cause. Often the nightmares result from a feeling of insecurity. Classically, the dreamer finds himself alone, running away from some inescapable tormentor. Occasionally worries about specific problems associated either with domestic upheavals or business problems may produce disturbing dreams which can be well described as nightmares.

The only real solution is rest and relief from pressure and the comfort of a reassuring and consistent domestic life. It is much easier to prescribe this solution than it is to provide it.

## Obesity

Overeating is a common response to anxiety (see p. 131) and anxiety is an almost inevitable consequence of overeating.

The dangers of obesity are well documented. Every organ in the body is under excessive and unnecessary strain when there is surplus fat to be carried around.

When overeating results from anxiety the solution is not simply obtaining a good diet although this may help. The victim must either find an alternative response to strain (such as nail biting – never likely to put on weight), learn to cope with pressure more effectively or organize his life so that he is exposed to less pressure.

## Obsessions

Most of us worry too much about quite ordinary things from time to time. We have probably all returned to the house to make sure the gas is turned off or gone downstairs at night to ensure that the back door is bolted. These are simply precautions taken by people who need reassurance before they can stop worrying. Nine time out of ten the gas will have been turned off and the back door will have been bolted.

Sometimes people find that they just cannot reassure themselves however many times they check to make sure that nothing is amiss. They go on worrying about it quite unreasonably, going back time and time again to check that the gas is off or the back door bolted. When this happens the sufferer is said to have an obsession.

It is often adult middle-aged women who develop obsessional neuroses and the person most likely to have to deal with an obsession will be the one who is normally quite rigid and stubborn in outlook. The woman who can't rest until all the cushions are tidy after a party, who gets the vacuum cleaner out after the visitors have gone, who rushes out after a small snow storm and sweeps the driveway clean. These are the early signs of a woman likely to develop obsessions later in her life. The problem often runs in families and a girl whose mother was obsessional may develop the same symptoms herself. No one really knows yet whether or not this is due to genetic or environmental factors.

Obsessions take many forms. The patient may need to bathe dozens of times in a day, may have to keep opening an envelope when a letter has been written to ensure that everything necessary has been said. And, of course, keeps checking that the doors and windows are locked and that taps and appliances are switched off. In the modern gadget-laden house there are many opportunities for obsesssions to develop.

Pressures and strains from the outside world often trigger off obsessional behaviour. The type of person who develops obsessions is likely to be uncertain and indecisive; they follow a rigid pattern of living and remain stubborn and resistant to change because of their fears of failure, inadequacy and insecurity. Psychiatrists explain obsessional behaviour in many different ways; usually basing their explanation on the theory that it is an interaction between the patient's personality and his immediate environment which results in the development of the obsession. The obsessions are tricks used by the mind to defend the individual from his own fears. Keep worrying about the back door and you'll have no time to worry about whether or not you're going to be evicted, divorced or sacked.

Although tranquillizers may help by reducing the effect of pressures and strains on the mind the best solution is simply to control the exposure to distress. The perfectionist who cannot rest until all is settled and neat and the stubborn who are always reluctant to accept new ideas or who find it difficult to adapt to change are poorly fitted for a life under strain. The development of obsessional ideas should be regarded as an early warning sign. The best and most permanent solution is to abstain from responsibility and to learn how to relax – particularly difficult for the patient who is obsessional because relaxing and taking things easy is likely to produce pangs of guilt.

The person who has an obsessional type of character, may, once the hazards of the character have been overcome, be extremely successful. The obsessional person will have a well-developed sense of duty, a feeling of responsibility and considerable determination. Obsessionals often prove admirable and successful administrators since they can be efficient and effective when dealing with predictable administrative problems.

## Overwork

Overwork may well be the factor responsible for producing numerous other disorders and it can itself be a disease needing treatment; although workaholics may not be as numerous as alcoholics they do have a right to receive attention and treatment.

People who work too much very rarely complain about having too much to do. Instead they will complain about not being able to do all that they feel they ought to be able to cope with. Usually self-employed, sometimes running their own business, often building up a professional practice, they may have genuine physical complaints such as gastric disturbances or cardiac troubles. They often complain of being unable to concentrate or sleep and their relatives may complain that they are bad tempered and impatient.

Trying to cope with their self-imposed workload while suffering from these ailments only makes things worse. As they get further and further behind with their targets they force themselves to work harder. Inevitably this makes things worse. Depression (see p. 149) and loss of memory may result. Major physical disasters, such as heart attacks (see p. 161) or bleeding ulcers (see p. 196) may intervene. A diminishing libido and impotence (p. 171) may be added to the list of symptoms associated with overwork.

Once the diagnosis has been made the solution is obvious.

### Palpitations
A palpitating heart is simply one that is beating unusually quickly. Normally the human heart beats at an average rate of about once a second although the precise figure varies from around 60 times a minute to 80 times a minute. Each time it beats the heart sends another supply of blood around the body to cope with the demands of the organs and tissues for food and oxygen and to collect and help dispose of waste materials.

The rate at which the heart beats has to be increased to cope with extra demands inspired by physical or mental exertion. If you run to catch a bus, enjoy an energetic half hour in bed or find yourself in the dock facing a charge of riding a bicycle without a working bell your heart will beat a little faster.

When the heart rate increases the owner may notice the difference and may even complain that his heart is thumping. Rather than being anything to worry about this is usually merely confirmation that the heart is doing its job properly. The only time to be worried about palpitations is if they occur accompanied by pain or a shortness of breath but if they occur frequently and without there being any logical explanation then ask your doctor about them.

### Phobias
Most of us have pet hates and dislikes. When those hates are so severe that we actually fear something and sweat with anxiety when confronted by it the fear is described as a phobia. Probably the best known phobia is claustrophobia. Most readers will

know of relatives or friends who suffer from this fear and who are terrified of enclosed spaces. There are various degrees of claustrophobia. Some sufferers cannot stand small confined spaces such as cupboards or lifts. The most severe sufferers will suffer acutely if threatened with enclosure in any small room.

Phobias are produced in many different ways. Sometimes a childhood experience can produce a fear which lasts through life. A mauling by a savage dog may, for example, produce a life-long phobia of all dogs. Sometimes phobias are produced as a defence mechanism to protect the patient from other fears. For example, a man who has lost his job and who feels that his status in society is so low that his colleagues and acquaintances may laugh at him if they see him may develop agoraphobia (a fear of going out into the open and moving about out of doors) and as a result may find in increasingly difficult to leave the house at all. Women whose husbands are away at work all day and who are climbing their social and professional ladder rapidly often develop agoraphobia if they feel that they are unable to hold their own with the wives of their husband's new colleagues.

Phobias nearly always result from some sort of situation which produces anxiety. The phobia is, of course, often nonsensical and the sufferer may well realize that it is nonsensical. That doesn't make it any easier to deal with. People who are afraid of spiders know in their hearts that few spiders are likely to prove dangerous – nevertheless the fear remains and may produce genuine symptoms of anxiety.

The most effective way for any sufferer to deal with their phobia is for them to try and de-condition themselves, preferably with the help and support of friends, relatives and fellow sufferers. The agoraphobic, for example, who is terrified of going out of doors should be helped out of the house slowly and in small stages. Begin by just opening the front door, then a few steps down the garden path, and then a little further. Similarly patients whose phobias concern cats should be encouraged to look at photographs of cats, to stroke simulated fur and to watch other people handling cats. Children who are exposed to situations likely to develop into phobias in later life should be encouraged to conquer their young fears as quickly as possible. Like the racing driver who climbs back into a car straight after a crash, and the jockey who gets on to a horse after falling, the child who falls out of a tree should be helped back into the tree with physical and mental support. If this doesn't happen a fear of heights may develop in later life.

Agoraphobia is the commonest and probably most limiting of all the phobias. It is estimated that in the United States there are 2.5 million agoraphobics. Over 2 million of these will be women. The psychological and physical explanations for agoraphobia are numerous, various and often startlingly inventive. Nevertheless it does seem true that like most other phobias it is often triggered off by strain and worry. To conquer it the sufferer has to deal both with the phobia and with any causative factors, such as an incident in childhood or a feeling of social insecurity.

Here is a list of some of the commonest phobias and the medical terms which describe them:

Acrophobia            fear of heights
Agoraphobia           fear of open spaces
Aichmophobia          fear of sharp objects
Ailurophobia          fear of cats
Algophobia            fear of pain
Anthropophobia        fear of people
Aquaphobia            fear of water
Brantophobia          fear of thunder
Cancerophobia         fear of cancer
Claustrophobia        fear of enclosed spaces
Cynophobia            fear of dogs
Demophobia            fear of crowds
Equinophobia          fear of horses
Herpetophobia         fear of creepy crawlies
Kainophobia           fear of new things
Mysophobia            fear of dirt
Nyctophobia           fear of the dark
Ophidophobia          fear of snakes
Phonophobia           fear of talking aloud
Pyrophobia            fear of fire
Schoolphobia          fear of going to school
Siderodromophobia     fear of travel

| Thanatophobia | fear of death |
| Xenophobia | fear of strangers |
| Zoophobia | fear of animals |

## Poisoning

Poisoning as a result of the swallowing of chemicals or drugs is a common cause of hospital admission. Accidental poisoning may occur when distress is so great that usual precautions are avoided or when senses are numbed either by grief or some self-administered anaesthetic to such an extent that a mistake is easily made. Many of those who take overdoses of sleeping tablets, for example, do so when already drowsy from a first dose.

Deliberate self-poisoning is invariably a direct result of distress and depression (see p. 149) and is a common method of suicide (see p. 191) and attempted suicide.

## Pregnancy

It may sound strange to describe pregnancy as a manifestation of stress but not infrequently a woman may deliberately allow herself to become pregnant in an attempt to escape from personal or environmental circumstances. To a married woman it may promise new strength for a fading marriage; to an unmarried woman it may promise some sort of escape route from hardship, drudgery or loneliness. Inevitably if the expected solution is not forthcoming the pregnancy may simply add to the problems which exist and the resultant baby may be the subject of mental or physical brutality (see p. 140).

## Psoriasis

Various parts of the body are affected by this skin disorder. If the disease affects the scalp the patient may complain of very bad dandruff. It is commonest on the elbows and knees and around the finger nails although it may attack other areas of the body. The skin has white patches which flake persistently and when the disease affects the elbows it seems like an attack of dandruff of the elbow.

About two per cent of the population have psoriasis. Most of the sufferers develop the diseases as teenagers, sometimes it runs in families but it may attack older people completely unexpectedly.

We don't know exactly what causes it but the usually accepted theories suggest that the skin cells produce new cells too quickly. In normal skin there is a permanent turn over of cells. As dead cells are sloughed off the surface of the skin so new ones form underneath. In psoriasis the production of new skin cells exceeds the sloughing off process. The disease is never contagious and affected skin can be handled without danger or risk by anyone.

The disorder isn't dangerous or disabling in any way but it is rarely curable. The problem is cosmetic rather than medical, although it is important to keep patches of psoriasis clean. They can easily become infected since there is no hard protective layer of well-developed skin cells to keep out infection. Doctors usually prescribe steroid creams and ointments for psoriasis sufferers and these products will help control the worst attacks. There are a number of organizations founded by and for sufferers of psoriasis which help with advice and information as well as ensuring a supply of funds to researchers interested in the disease. Psoriasis is most common in cold damp countries; it is relatively rare in dry climates. Extreme heat, however, is likely to make an existing case of psoriasis worse. The best climate seems to be that of a fairly good northern European summer!

Occasionally, first attacks of psoriasis are triggered off by physical illness but most commonly it is anxiety or nervous tension that produces the initial and subsequent attacks. Sufferers often notice that attacks occur at moments of crisis throughout their lives. A bad attack will settle best if a holiday or period of comparative peace follows as quickly as possible. Like angina (see p. 126) and indigestion (see p. 172), psoriasis is an early warning sign that the body has reached its stress threshold.

**Puerperal depression**
It is extremely common for a woman who has just given birth to a baby to feel depressed during the first few days of mother-

hood. The puerperal blues as the depression is called is usually over in a day or so and invariably occurs towards the end of the first week after the birth of the baby.

When the depression doesn't lift quickly it needs to be taken more seriously. Pregnancy puts a woman under a considerable strain. She may worry about her own health, about the likelihood of her baby being born with a congenital disorder, about the prospect of a painful delivery, about her own competence to look after a child and about her ability to retain her husband's affection as her shape changes and her commitments increase. It is this accumulation of strains and pressures which cause the post-parturition blues and not any special disease process; hormonal changes may be influential but it is the accumulation of fears, hopes and expectations that is really responsible. There is in addition a feeling of anticlimax after the birth.

Inevitably it is women who are prone to attacks of anxiety or uncertainty or who lack confidence in themselves who are most likely to develop depression after giving birth. Reassurance, therefore, is a vital part of the necessary treatment. Tranquillizers and anti-depressants may be needed and if prescribed will usually need to be taken for at least a month before they will help. If the new mother can be convinced that she is capable and that things will prove manageable then the depression will lift all the quicker. The baby may occasionally need to be taken away and cared for outside the home for a few days or perhaps weeks if the mother's depression is very deep.

When you consider the number of anxieties, fears and potential problems likely to trouble the pregnant woman it is a tribute to the female of the species that not more young mothers are affected by puerperal depression.

Any mother who is depressed for more than two or three days at a time after childbirth should see her doctor immediately.

## Rheumatic diseases

There are over a hundred different types of rheumatic disease, each needing a specific type of treatment. Rheumatoid arthritis is probably the commonest member of this group of ailments; it affects millions of people around the world and is a long-lasting disease which progresses at varying rates and most frequently starts in middle or later life.

In rheumatoid arthritis, the synovium, which is a fine smooth tissue which surrounds the ends of the two bones forming a joint, becomes inflamed. The inflammation causes swelling of the joint and fluid collects inside the synovium and around the bones. If the inflammation is not controlled, then the joint becomes weaker, less mobile, and is eventually effectively destroyed.

Doctors still do not know why the inflammation starts, although some blame a virus which is a member of the same family as the bug which causes the common cold.

Treatment of joints affected by rheumatoid arthritis (and most of the joints in the body *can* be involved) involves drugs such as the well-established aspirin and the more recently introduced steroid drugs, gentle exercise and physiotherapy, heat treatment and the use of artificial aids and even surgery.

Another major rheumatism disorder is *osteoarthritis*. This disease is particularly common in older people. By the age of seventy nearly everyone has some osteoarthritis, although most do not have the pain or stiffness which goes with the disorder. The cartilage, which covers the end of each bone, gradually breaks up and disappears, leaving the raw ends of bone grating on each other. Osteoarthritis usually affects the larger joints such as the knees or hips and for these, surgeons can provide artificial joints which restore the mobility lost when the cartilage disappears. It's often not realized that the human backbone consists of a number of bones, separated by joints which depend upon cartilage for mobility. The cartilage is the soft, rubbery substance which allows bones to move freely over one another. In the spine, as in the knees, this cartilage can disappear leaving a creaking back.

*Gout* is another well-known disease in the same group and although traditionally thought to hit only heavy drinkers, gout does, in fact, affect many other people too. It is caused by the deposition of uric arid crystals in the joints, and there are a number of drugs available which help cut down the level of this acid in the blood and therefore reduce the symptoms of gout.

*Ankylosing spondylitis* is a rheumatic disease of the spine which most commonly affects men in their twenties or thirties. The symptoms are usually low back pain since it is usually the lower part of the back which is affected first of all.

Another rheumatic disease which causes pain and deformity, which affects the finger and toe joints, and which is associated with the skin disease called psoriasis, is called *psoriatic arthritis.* Then there is a disease called *Reiter's Syndrome* which involves arthritic attacks in many joints and inflammation of the eyes and the skin. All these diseases are slightly different but all have much in common – they are members of the same family.

*Rheumatic fever*, the disease which follows infection with a bug called streptococcus, affects children and damages the heart. During the rheumatic fever many joints are affected but it is the changes in the heart valves which cause the greatest problems in later life. Incidentally, chorea or St Vitus Dance, as it is also known, is a complication of rheumatic fever.

Although we have managed to define all these different diseases we still know very little about what causes many of them. If, as some doctors suspect, the inflammatory processes of rheumatoid arthritis are triggered off by a virus which is a relative of the cold causing virus then it is very likely that strains and distresses will exacerbate a mild condition or accelerate the development of one. Exposure to troublesome, long-standing problems undoubtedly reduces the resistance of an otherwise healthy individual and increases the likelihood of a rheumatic disease developing.

## Sexual problems

The quality and quantity of sexual enjoyment we obtain from our relationship with others is not only a cause of much anxiety and a direct producer of distress but is also affected by strains and distresses produced by other completely unconnected factors. The ability to achieve sexual success and satisfaction is greatly influenced by the mental state of both partners.

Firstly, there are the worries and anxieties produced by a lack of self-confidence both in one's own ability and in the satisfac-

187

tory state of one's equipment. Men worry about the size of their penises, women worry about the shape of their breasts, the size of their buttocks and the capacity of their vaginas. Members of both sexes worry about their general attractiveness to prospective partners.

Failure to climax, to bring a partner to orgasm or to be able to repeat a satisfactory performance at short notice and without adequate rest are also sources of discontent. Worry about possible pain inflicted, about pain to be experienced or about a lack of pain can also produce anxiety. People worry about having it too often or not often enough; about being too creative or not being daring enough. When it comes to sex almost anything is a possible source of distress.

Worry about performance and over eagerness produce two types of problems which may also occur as a result of extraneous worries which have nothing at all to do with sex. Both these problems concern the male since whatever problems the female of the species may have are rarely likely to be immediately obvious to her partner. A woman can disguise and camouflage her own lack of satisfaction and may be able to satisfy a man without satisfying herself. The male, with a role requiring more than willingness may find himself embarrassed by failure.

Premature ejaculation is a phrase used to describe a male orgasm which occurs too soon. Usually this problem is caused by sexual anxieties or by unbridled enthusiasm. Inexperience or lack of practice may both lead to premature ejaculation. It is important to realize that this is a problem which can be solved and is not a permanent disability. Experience may help but occasionally ejaculation may be too rapid even after plentiful practice. Anaesthetic creams are sometimes recommended to delay orgasm but the same effect can often be obtained by learning to control the rate at which an orgasm approaches. A willing and helpful partner is needed to help reduce stimuli. Minimal movement may help lengthen the lifespan of an erection. It is important to remember that an erection which follows soon after a premature ejaculation is likely to last much longer and prove more satisfactory than the first one.

The second problem which sometimes interferes is impotence (see p. 171). All men are impotent at one time or another.

Sometimes the cause is purely sexual. The male is too anxious to impress or on the other hand he may be bored by his partner whom he no longer finds attractive. Too rich a sex life may leave even the most enthusiastic stud with a limp and half useless weapon. Sometimes the cause is physical. Drugs used for patients with hypertension, alcohol, and some hormonal diseases all contribute. The commonest cause, however, is worry.

## Strokes

The brain, like all other organs, has a plentiful supply of blood vessels. The arteries which bring fresh oxygenated blood from the lungs criss-cross the brain tissue to provide a comprehensive supply service. If any one of these arteries become blocked by a blood clot or if the pressure within an artery becomes so great that a wall is ruptured allowing blood to leak into the surrounding brain tissue than there will be inevitable damage done. The amount of damage depends partly upon the site of the mishap and partly upon its size. A small clot which blocks off a minor artery may produce little more than a paralysis of the fingers of one hand. A major clot which blocks off a main artery can be fatal.

Once a stroke has occurred all is by no means lost. Recovery often takes place and a patient who seemed paralysed one day may within a few weeks be walking and talking as if nothing had happened. The human body has tremendous powers of recovery even from apparently enormous calamities.

The body's own power of recovery can be aided and boosted by active intervention. After a stroke a patient is likely to be confused and to have a limp, apparently powerless muscles. Sensation may have been lost and the patient may not be able to see or to speak. A patient recovering from a stroke should be encouraged to work hard to regain the use of limbs and the power of speech. Exercises, both for the body and the mind are essential and where there are residual weaknesses special equipment can be obtained to help give the partly disabled aid with chores and tasks. In my book *Everything you want to know about ageing* (Gordon & Cremonesi, 1976) I describe in considerable detail the ways in which a patient with a stroke can be helped.

The following table shows occupational influences on deaths caused by strokes. A standardized mortality ratio of 100 would be an average for all workers. (Figures from the Registrar General's Occupational Mortality tables.)

| | | |
|---|---|---|
| Company directors | 485 | |
| Coalmine face workers | 229 | |
| Unskilled workers (general) | 166 | |
| Dockers | 153 | above average |
| Telephone operators | 129 | |
| Doctors | 110 | |
| Ships' officers, pilots | 110 | |
| Civil Servants | 107 | |
| | | |
| Carpenters | 98 | |
| Accountants | 92 | |
| Gardeners, groundsmen | 90 | |
| Foresters, woodsmen | 90 | |
| MPs, senior govt. officers | 86 | |
| Electricians | 86 | below average |
| Lawyers | 84 | |
| Shop assistants | 84 | |
| Clergy | 83 | |
| Teachers | 58 | |
| Authors | 42 | |
| Secretaries, typists | 36 | |

## Stuttering

Stuttering, or stammering as it is known, is to conversation what impotence is to sex. Both are symptoms of anxiety and both are best cured by treating the underlying anxiety. There are said to be 2.6 million stutterers in the United States of America and half a million sufferers in Britain. Members of the British royal family, politicians and even figures in the entertainment business have all suffered from the indignity of being unable to say what they want to say.

There are just about as many explanations for stuttering as there are psychologists and psychiatrists in the western world and there are thousands of recommended techniques and gadgets said to be of help to those who suffer. The truth is that no one knows precisely what causes stuttering although everyone agrees that social strains and pressures make it worse and that when anxious to please or impress the stutterer is likely to make an even greater mess of his words than usual.

For the speaker who does not normally stammer at all an inability to enunciate clearly may be an early warning sign of a build up of pressure. The long-suffering stammerer who can never speak without difficulty is likely to suffer when social strains are mild and not threatening. There is no easy solution although some people may find that one or other of the 'magical' remedies suits them. Perhaps the best answer for the stutterer whose affliction is newly acquired is simply a reduction in the level of pressure endured.

## Suicide

A survey at a major London teaching hospital has recently shown that one in every five of the people admitted to the medical wards of the hospital need treatment because they have tried to kill themselves. It is clearly obvious that suicide is not something that can be ignored as 'unpleasant' or 'unlikely to affect my family'. Suicides and attempted suicides are more common in some hospitals than road traffic accident victims, patients with cancer or pneumonia or patients who have had heart attacks. And the rate at which suicide attempts take place is continuing to increase. In particular the number who take overdoses of drugs is rising. It has been estimated that if the present rate of increase is maintained by 1984 everyone in the country will take an overdose of drugs at least once a year. A frightening thought.

Most disturbing is the fact that a great many attempted suicides involve teenagers, and indeed children who are hardly out of their first decade.

There are two questions which any parent will want to ask when confronted with the fact that teenagers are common suicide victims. What sort of pressures are involved and how can they be alleviated? And how can any parent tell if their child is so depressed that suicide is a real danger?

The answer to the first question is simply that teenagers today are under tremendous pressures from many different areas. To begin with they are of course under pressure from the changes which their own hormonal development produces.

The girl who is slightly more or less shapely than her school-friends or the boy who is taller or shorter than most of his contemporaries will both be under unusual strains. To these traditional problems must be added the educational and social pressures which are more peculiar to our time. More and more young people are expected to stay on at school, and to acquire academic qualifications. Naturally a good number of these young people find academic work difficult. They try to please parents and teachers but may find it exceedingly difficult. At sixteen many youngsters are looking for work. Frequently they are unable to find it. There are in addition the problems of dealing with conflicting advice and exhortations from family and friends of the same age. At sixteen young people are often expected to be responsible but rarely given any real responsibility. At a time when many youngsters are still developing their own personality they may also be acquiring a family of their own. Even though many young people postpone marriage until mid or late twenties there are many thousands who for one reason or another have family responsibilities in their teens.

What can parents do to help their children through these difficult years? Well, perhaps most important of all, they can understand that their children *are* growing up and need to be considered as young adults rather than as elderly children. They should try to give their offspring some responsibility, even though they may still be at school. Restrictions should be practical, sensible and, if possible, discussed. All age groups have their fashions and fads and these signs of self-expression should be accepted as such. The parent who categorically denies their son or daughter the opportunity to follow some fashions will be storing up future trouble.

Parents should try to get into the habit of discussing problems with children as they mature. Reasoned explanations are better than bald orders. Encourage children to talk about the pressures which they feel exist and try not to dismiss fears which you know are unreal or unjustified out of hand.

As to the second question, 'How do I know if my child is depressed to such an extent that suicide or attempted suicide is a real possibility?' there *are* some pointers.

The teenager who isn't eating properly (see p. 129) or who is eating too much, who has difficulty in sleeping, who spends no time at all with friends, who is irritable and whose life pattern changes noticeably may be at risk. The teenager who used to be concerned about housework but who forgets to do it or who simply doesn't bother may need help. When there are symptoms like this then offer to talk or insist upon a visit to the family doctor. If necessary talk to teachers or friends. Don't wait until it is too late.

Suicide is, of course, by no means confined to teenagers. The warning signs which may precede a suicide attempt are similar in people of different ages. In the section of the book on depression (see p. 149) I describe in greater detail some of the symptoms likely to give a friend or relative a chance to intervene before suicide is attempted. There is an erroneous theory that people who talk about suicide never actually attempt it. That isn't true. Anyone who talks about suicide should see a doctor straightaway. And until they have received medical help they should never be left alone. There are two reasons for this. Firstly, it helps a depressed person to have someone around and secondly, the attendant may be able to physically prevent a suicide attempt.

Pills are the commonest weapon of the suicide victim and women make up three quarters of all those who attempt it.

The table that follows shows occupational influences on death by suicide. A standardized mortality ratio of 100 would be an average for all workers. (Figures from the Registrar General's Occupational Mortality tables.)

| | | |
|---|---|---|
| Company directors | 1925 | |
| Civil Servants | 446 | |
| Authors | 200 | |
| Unskilled workers (general) | 184 | |
| Doctors | 176 | |
| Lawyers | 133 | above average |
| Telephone operators | 129 | |
| Gardeners, groundsmen | 119 | |
| Dockers | 114 | |
| Ships' officers, pilots | 111 | |
| Electricians | 111 | |
| Carpenters | 101 | |

| | | |
|---|---|---|
| Secretaries, typists | 100 | average |
| Shop assistants | 100 | |
| | | |
| Teachers | 94 | |
| Foresters, woodsmen | 93 | |
| Accountants | 91 | below average |
| Coalmine face workers | 73 | |
| Clergy | 53 | |
| MPs, senior govt. officers | 30 | |

### Thyroid disorders

Thyroid disorders can be divided into two main groups: there are those caused by the fact that the gland is producing too much hormone and there are those caused by the gland not producing enough thyroid hormone.

There are many reasons for an enlarged or overactive thyroid gland but Asher and Flack in 1910 and Rahe, Rogers, Fawcett and Beebe in 1914 showed that thyroid secretion can be stimulated by the nervous system. The symptoms usually include irritability, an inability to tolerate hot weather or to sit still for more than a few minutes, a hearty appetite coupled with a persistent loss of weight, a tendency to cry for no reason at all and an increase in the amount of sweat produced. Thyrotoxic women are likely to fail to have normal menstrual periods for several months at a time. The overactive thyroid gland produces several obvious signs which can be identified by any intelligent observer. Firstly, of course, there is the swelling in the neck. There may be protruding eyes with the whites showing above and below the iris. Thyrotoxic people are usually thin.

There are several reasons why thyroid glands may fail to produce enough thyroid hormone. There may have been a shortage of tissue at birth or the gland may simply fail to function normally or it may have been removed surgically to treat a case of thyrotoxicosis. The symptoms of myxoedema, the opposite of thyrotoxicosis, are roughly speaking the opposite to the symptoms associated with an excess of thyroid hormone. Patients cannot stand the cold, they put on lots of extra weight although they don't eat much, they spend most of their time sitting around doing nothing and they develop gruff voices and dry skin and hair.

The myxoedematous patient is unlikely to react to pressure or strain. He is far too lethargic to bother when things are going wrong. The thyrotoxic patient, on the other hand, will worry and fret when things are going well. When there are problems he or she (and most thyrotoxic patients are female) will find life almost intolerable. Any sort of distress will make a thyrotoxic patient suffer greatly.

Patients with thyroid disorders can often be treated very effectively. Thyrotoxic patients may benefit from drugs or surgery. Myxodematous patients may get better when given thyroid hormone tablets to take.

### Tremors

A tremor is an involuntary and usually rhythmical movement of a group of muscles and it is a symptom rather than a disease. When stimuli from the world outside are pouring into an already overworked central nervous system the communications system between nerves and muscles shows signs of overloading. Under normal circumstances voluntary muscles only operate when they receive impulses passed down from the brain or spinal cord. When a person is under a great deal of strain, however, the number of impulses travelling along the nerves may prove too much for the system to cope with. Rather in the way that a nervous pedestrian may panic if caught in the middle of the road between opposite streams of traffic and step first one way and then the other way so the muscles which are normally under voluntary control will twitch and tremble, uncertain about whether to move this way or that or to simply keep still.

### Tumours

Some doctors believe that cancers can be produced as a result of an immune response within the body. Those who follow this theory argue that subjects who are particularly susceptible to pressure are more likely to develop tumours produced by auto-immune responses.

On a more practical level there is absolutely no doubt that a victim who responds to pressure by smoking more heavily will increase his likelihood of developing lung cancer. I do not think it is stretching the point too far to say that the pressure has indirectly produced the cancer.

## Ulcers

The terms peptic ulcer, gastric ulcer and duodenal ulcer are often used indiscriminately and as if they were interchangeable. So I want to begin this section by explaining just what these three phrases mean.

The phrase peptic ulcer simply refers to any ulcer, or surface defect, in the upper part of the intestinal tract. A peptic ulcer may be in the stomach, duodenum or even the oesophagus. The term gastric ulcer refers specifically to an ulcer present in the stomach while when doctors talk about duodenal ulcers, they are referring to ulcers in the duodenum – the stretch of bowel which follows on from the stomach.

It is the stomach's job to turn the vast variety of foodstuffs dropped into it into a moveable thick soup and to facilitate this process the cells of the stomach lining produce a total of something like three litres of gastric juice a day. The muscles of the stomach wall churn food and juices together before squirting the resultant mixture through a valve into the duodenum. The most important constituent of the gastric juice is hydrochloric acid; an acid strong enough to burn holes in your carpet if accidentally spilt.

The secretion of gastric juices is started by a number of stimulants. Hunger, alcohol, nicotine and stress all produce impulses which are carried by the vagus nerve to the stomach without the owner's knowledge, then those impulses result in the flow of gastric juices within the stomach. If too much acid is produced then ulcers may develop.

We do not know a great deal about just why ulcers develop in some people but not in others, but we do know that they run in families and that if your father or mother had an ulcer there is a greater chance that you will have one.

We also know that ulcers are more common in people usually referred to as middle-aged. There is no firm evidence to show that a person's physique or personality affects his or her likelihood to develop an ulcer and indeed although there are statistics to suggest that the ulcer victim will be a middle-aged man, seven year old boys and seventy year old women can develop ulcers as well.

Gastric ulcers tend to occur in older people whereas duodenal ulcers usually affect younger people. Gastric ulcers occur in both men and women, whereas duodenal ulcers, with little regard for the womens' liberation movement, seem to prefer male bowels. Duodenal ulcers are, in bold statistical terms, four times as common in men as in women.

Duodenal ulcers occur in all social classes though, if anything, there is a preponderance of ulcer victims among the professional groups. On the other hand, gastric ulcers are commoner among working class people. Gastric ulcers are relatively rare in the speedboat and barbecue bracket.

The most important, and often the only, symptom of peptic ulceration is the pain, which is usually localized in the epigastrium, a point half way between the chin and umbilicus and right in the centre of the chest. The characteristics of the pain sometimes help doctors to differentiate between gastric ulcers and duodenal ulcers. People who have a duodenal ulcer usually find that their pain is relieved when they eat, whereas people with gastric ulceration usually find that their pain comes on after meals. Patients with duodenal ulcers often wake at night and find that if they eat a biscuit and drink a glass of milk their pain will go away. Indeed, duodenal ulcer pain comes and goes a great deal; it may go away for several months at a time and just as the patient is beginning to think he is entirely free of trouble, back it will come. It is this periodic nature of the pain which makes duodenal ulcers an easy target for unscrupulous medicine makers. The medicine may seem to work but the pain might well have disappeared anyway.

The only other symptoms of peptic ulceration are usually water-brash, that is the filling of the mouth with a tasteless watery sort of saliva, and vomiting. The vomiting, incidentally, may well relieve the pain of an ulcer.

Though the types of pain I have described are usually pretty indicative of an ulcer, if you visit your doctor and complain of this type of pain he may want to arrange a barium meal examination. This is an investigation which involves the drinking of an opaque mixture which will show up on an X-ray. When the mixture goes into the stomach the radiologist, the doctor who takes and studies X-ray films, will be able to see if there are any ulcerated marks on either the stomach or duodenal walls.

There is a traditional belief that the right diet will take care of a peptic ulcer, and there are, around the world, many thousands of people religiously living on a diet of steamed fish and blancmange because a once fashionable theory was that peptic ulcers could be cured by the right sort of dietary habits. I'm afraid that those poor people are punishing themselves quite unnecessarily. A light, milky diet will certainly help relieve the symptoms of peptic ulceration but it will not cure an ulcer.

There are several things which can be done in the acute stages of ulcer pain. The patient should be sent to bed, told to stay in bed and to do as little as possible. He should not be given access to a telephone and not allowed to have any worrying news. He should be forbidden spicy foods, cigarettes and alcohol and given a two hourly diet of milky foods, since these will help relieve the pain by counteracting the effects of excess acid. Antacids, either bought from a pharmacist or obtained from a doctor on prescription will also help relieve symptoms.

When a bad attack of pain is over the patient should give up smoking permanently, avoid foods which he knows will upset him (spicy and greasy foods in particular), drink only in moderation and learn to relax (see p. 89) and cope with potentially stressful situations.

The effects of stress on the stomach lining were well illustrated by two sets of experiments done in the USA. In the 1830s an American surgeon, William Beaumont, recorded his observations of an Indian called Alexis St Martin, who had been wounded by a gun and left with a fistula which enabled observers to view his stomach lining. Later another doctor employed a technician called Tom who had part of his stomach visible and repeated the observations. Both doctors confirmed that anger, fear, and other emotional states affected the stomach lining and caused an outpouring of acid. These observers also noted that when calm and relaxed the amount of acid produced diminished with the result that the mucosa took on a much healthier appearance.

Since peptic ulcers, and in particular duodenal ulcers often occur as a direct result of stress it is clear that reducing stress may also prove an excellent way of either hastening the healing of an ulcer or preventing the development of an ulcer. Remove your exposure to stress by changing your life style and your first ulcer may well disappear, while your second may never appear.

There are a number of drugs, both freely available over the chemist's counter and available only on prescription, which are said to help 'heal' ulcers. There is yet no real evidence to show that any product can offer improvement as real as that obtained by a change in life style, although simple antacids do provide temporary symptomatic relief.

Patients often ask about the advantages of having surgery for an ulcer. It is certainly not justifiable to have an operation after a single attack of ulcer pain. The proper treatment of bed rest, a milky diet, antacids and a change in unhealthy habits may be sufficient to provide a temporary if not a permanent cure. If the pains persist, recur and prove genuinely incapacitating then an operation may prove a boon. There are several types of operation done for an ulcer. In some cases the ulcer itself and part of the stomach wall are simply removed. In other cases the nerves supplying the stomach and influencing the outflow of acid are cut.

There are two major complications likely to result from peptic ulceration. Firstly, the ulcer may erode an artery in the intestinal wall with a resultant haemorrhage within the intestines. If the blood passes through the intestines it will be black (melaena); if vomited out it will appear dark brown (haematemesis). Vomited blood from a bleeding ulcer is usually described as having the appearance of coffee grounds. A patient who has passed or vomited blood will probably be pale, faint and sweaty. He needs urgent medical help. Similarly a patient whose ulcer has perforated through the duodenal or stomach wall should also receive urgent help. There will be little doubt about the need for emergency treatment when an ulcer has perforated for the patient will be in considerable pain.

The table below shows occupational influences on deaths caused by duodenal ulcer. A standardized mortality ratio of 100 would be an average for all workers. (Figures from the Registrar General's Occupational Mortality tables.)

| | | |
|---|---:|---|
| Company directors | 700 | |
| Coalmine face workers | 200 | |
| Unskilled workers (general) | 193 | |
| Dockers | 150 | above average |
| Carpenters | 133 | |
| Ships' officers, pilots | 125 | |
| Civil Servants | 125 | |
| | | |
| Telephone operators | 100 | |
| Secretaries, typists | 100 | |
| Authors | 100 | average |
| Lawyers | 100 | |
| Shop assistants | 100 | |
| | | |
| Gardeners, groundsmen | 81 | |
| Teachers | 80 | |
| Foresters, woodsmen | 75 | |
| Doctors | 67 | below average |
| Clergy | 60 | |
| Electricians | 50 | |
| MPs, senior govt. officers | 44 | |
| Accountants | 31 | |

## Vomiting

Vomiting may be a sign of acute distress. Sudden exposure to gory sights may produce vomiting. For example, seeing a street accident may make a passer-by actually sick. The phrase, 'You make me sick' is well established in colloquial English. Usually this type of vomiting happens only occasionally and is not persistent. Very occasionally, however, particularly anxious or distressed individuals may vomit persistently for long periods.

Nausea and vomiting are usually symptoms of acute, severe

anxiety attacks rather than of long-lasting chronic anxiety. Because the vomiting attacks are unpredictable and are usually caused by unplanned anxieties or fears there is no really effective way of preventing them. The only common after effects of fear-induced vomiting are embarrassment and a hefty dry cleaning bill.

# Appendix
## The Mechanism of Stress

# INTRODUCTION

There are literally hundreds of physiology text books available which describe in detail exactly how the body reacts when provoked, surprised or subjected to any notable stimulus.

This short appendix is not intended to be a substitute for those texts nor even a precis of what they contain. My intention is solely to provide the interested reader with a brief and inevitably imprecise general account of the mechanisms through which stimuli from the environment and feelings originating within the brain itself can initiate physiological responses and produce direct physical damage. The reader who merely wishes to take advantage of the counterstress philosophy needs this small section of the book no more than the consumer wishing to drive a new motor car or operate a new stereo system needs to understand the technical developments and theoretical laws which make possible the machinery he operates.

## The arrival of information

Every second of every minute of every day of your life your nervous system receives about a hundred million messages, travelling at about 675 mph. Those messages come from every part of your body. Clearly, the less important messages have to be ignored, or at least put on one side while the urgent problems are dealt with. And that is exactly what your brain does. As you read this you are breathing but you are not aware that your lungs are functioning; you are perhaps digesting your last meal but, unless something is going wrong, you will not be aware of the digestive processes. If you are concentrating properly your mind will be cutting out extraneous information gathered by your special senses systems. You will, for example, be able to ignore the sounds of the clock ticking and the refrigerator humming.

Apart from messages provided by the senses (hearing, sight, smell, taste and touch), there are impulses from numerous receptors hidden deep inside the body. There are visceroreceptors which tell you what your internal organs are doing at any particular time. Chemoreceptors telling you what sort of chemical condition your blood is in and proprioceptors telling you what your muscles and tendons are doing. In addition there are, of course, messages from higher brain centres. Anticipation, thought, memory and other types of thinking produce impulses.

Of course, any particular stimulus can produce an infinite variety of other stimuli. For example, there will be a psychological effect and a physiological result. The psychological result may produce in turn other psychological feelings. The physiological result may produce psychological reactions of its own and vice versa. For example, if a woman takes her child into town with her and sees him nearly run over by a motor car because she's been busily gazing into a shop window and hasn't been able to keep a proper eye on him, she will be full of confused reactions. She will experience a physiological reaction as she automatically feels anxious to help. Her body will prepare itself for the emergency her ears and eyes tell her exists. She will feel guilty about neglecting the child and frightened for its safety as well as happy that it has not been injured. She may feel a sharp pain in her chest because of the distress and this may convince her that she is about to have a heart attack. All these stimuli will clamour for some sort of action. The result may be such total confusion that the woman just stands there on the pavement and does nothing. She may not even cry. Her only reaction may be an automatic half stifled cry of despair.

Many of the messages which travel to your brain never produce any reaction at all. Reactions only occur when the intensity of a sensation is considerable; and the intensity of a sensation depends upon the frequency at which impulses are received. Identical stimuli of equal potency may, of course, produce different results and different lesions in different people. The effects any stimulus has depends upon the age, sex and genetic makeup of the individual as well as upon the intake of drugs, diet and alcohol and the general physical status. For example, in old age there is a loss of adaptability to stimuli. The old suffer more when confronted with some stimuli, but suffer less when confronted with others.

The fact that impulses are ignored does not mean that they stop coming. On the contrary they never stop coming whatever is happening. The central nervous system is kept permanently up to date with information from touch receptors, organs of taste, smell, sight and hearing and from special receptors in the internal organs, the blood vessels and muscles.

## Automatic responses – when your body knows best

Much of the information which the brain receives is processed without your ever being consciously aware of it having even arrived. Numerous information-collecting agencies throughout the body keep the brain permanently supplied with up to date information on the temperature of the environment, the state of the body's water and oxygen supplied and the position and state of the muscles and joints around the body.

The human body is like one of those dolls with the lead filled bases, which rock back into position when buffeted. Numerous automatic defence mechanisms and regulatory agencies are permanently available to protect the body from potentially dangerous environmental variations. These inbuilt protective mechanisms are vitally important for the human body is a delicate and sensitive organism which operates effectively only when certain basic internal conditions are met.

The remarkable nature of these defence mechanisms is well illustrated by the fact that although the human body can only survive when the temperature of the blood and body remains well between 30 and 45 degrees centigrade, human beings survive when the temperature in the environment is much hotter or much colder than this. The body's warning system, defence mechanisms and protective equipment enable it to adapt to such rapidly changing conditions. It is these defence mechanisms which enable the Eskimo to survive in his igloo, the African tribesman to survive in the bush and the Arab to stay alive in the desert.

The body maintains its stable internal environment by modifying its physical structure to suit the external environment. For example, when a man is stranded in the desert his surface blood vessels dilate so that his skin turns bright pink. The superficial blood flow enables his body to lose considerable quantities of heat. Even more heat is lost by the body's cunning use of the fact that when water evaporates, heat is lost. Just as people in hot climates keep their butter cool by storing it in water filled porous pots, which allow water to evaporate, so the human body loses heat by sweating. When the sweat evaporates heat is lost into the surrounding air. People sweating automatically produce less saliva, have dry mouths, become thirsty and drink. This ensures that the body's attempts to keep its temperature down do not result in a dangerous loss of necessary fluids. The body has another technique available to help it to lose heat. On breathing out, heat is lost on the breath. This is why dogs pant on hot days. Humans do the same but less dramatically. Incidentally, the body produces less heat when it is still and so the natural response of a human being who is hot is to lie still.

When, on the other hand, the body is surrounded by cold air, the surface blood vessels constrict, so reducing the flow of blood through the skin. The surface hairs on the body stand up in a vain attempt to keep a layer of warm air trapped next to the skin. (In man, who has long since lost his hairy coat, cold weather merely produces goose pimples.) You shiver because this involves your muscles in physical activity which produces heat; you may even automatically stamp your feet to produce more heat.

Blood is a vital bodily constituent. It carries oxygen from the lungs to the tissues and removes waste products. Without a steady flow of blood the human body cannot work. When blood is lost the human body employs a number of techniques to ensure that whatever supply is left is utilized properly, rather in the way that the electricity board tries to ensure that vital services continue to get supplies of electricity in times of short supply. It is the brain and the heart which must continue to be supplied properly and to ensure that this happens the body reduces the size of the vessels supplying the muscles and skin. At the same time the size of the vessels supplying the brain and the heart is increased. In addition, fluid flows out of the tissues into the blood to help keep the blood volume at a good level (the shortage of tissue fluid incidentally produces a feeling of thirst which automatically helps to restore the lost fluids) and if there is a leak in the system at any point an automatic clotting mechanism comes into operation after giving the local blood vessels a chance to wash out any invading germs. The loss of fluid through the kidneys is also temporarily reduced.

When oxygen is in short supply, as it is for example at high altitudes, the body reacts in several ways to ensure that the supply reaching working organs is maintained at a good level. The number of blood corpuscles is increased and the muscles pump the corpuscles round the body at a faster rate. The heart beats faster and increases its output every time it beats. Thus, although each corpuscle carries less oxygen than usual, the supply is nearly normal.

These mechanisms all help to maintain the body's status quo despite changes in the general environment. There are, in addition, a number of automatic responses which protect the body from any number of more specific potential hazards.

If someone mischievously tickles the end of your nose with a feather you'll probably sneeze, because of a reflex designed to help you to expel foreign bodies from inside your nostrils. Should this reflex fail to operate properly and allow some foreign body to find its way through the nose, and into the throat then you will cough. At the same time as the cough reflex is triggered off you will automatically swallow so that anything coughed up can be swept down the oesophagus and into the stomach. If the object is too big to be swallowed you will gag and the object will come flying out again; if it is poisonous then the stomach will probably reject it and you will be sick. If you put something into your mouth which is an irritant the saliva will fairly pour out of your salivary glands. If you walk into a sand storm your eyelids will automatically close to protect your eyes and the tears will flow in abundance to wash out your eyes and keep the conjunctiva clean. Sit on a nail and you'll jump up because the sensation of pain automatically takes you away from the stimulus. If you swallow threatening bacteria you will develop vomiting and diarrhoea as your body tries to expel the dangerous invader. The intestines will wriggle and writhe as they attempt to hurry the invaders through. Drink a great deal of water and your kidneys will automatically allow a good supply of weak urine to leave the body. Drink too little and the kidneys will automatically concentrate the urine so that little water is lost. Eat too much salt and the excess will be excreted in the urine.

If you do regular heavy work your skin will become thicker and rougher so that it is more capable of coping with the heavy work. Callouses may develop to protect the skin. Contract an infectious disease and your body temperature will rise to try and kill off the causative organisms. Minor skin infections are sealed off as boils and your tonsils act as barriers preventing bacteria from getting into the body. Lose blood and you faint so that your brain becomes level with your heart rather than above it and receives as good a blood supply as possible. After heavy exercise when you have used up stocks of sugar you will feel hungry. The empty stomach contracts and eventually goes into spasm. These are hunger pangs, which are relieved by eating. The full stomach sends back a signal which results in a feeling of satiation.

These accurate, automatic responses should show that our body does, indeed, know best. Unhappily, we rarely appreciate the efforts that our bodies make on our behalf. We damage our ability to respond to environmental changes by allowing our protective mechanisms to atrophy and by deliberately overriding them in the same way that office workers sometimes wedge open fire doors because it is more convenient. When we have an attack of bacteria-induced diarrhoea we take medicines to stop it. When we feel full we still eat more. When we develop boils we put creams on to them to simply send the bacteria running back for cover instead of breaking out into the open where they can easily be removed. When we feel hot, instead of allowing our bodies to look after the problem for us, we impatiently eat icecream and install air conditioning. When we feel cold we install central heating.

When we sweat we use powders and deodorants. When our hair grows we cut it off; when callouses develop we soften them; when tonsils do their job we have them removed; when the temperature rises during an infection we bring it down with drugs. As a result of our cunning we develop many new and more disturbing disorders. We get colds, and our infections last longer. It really is a pity that we do not realize just what our bodies do for us and acknowledge that in some circumstances our bodies do know best.

### State of alert

Some information requires immediate attention and the body's automatic defence mechanisms cannot cope with it alone. If, for example, you are standing in a quiet room where you think you are alone and totally unexpectedly a plate falls onto the hard floor directly behind you, having been dislodged by an intruding cat, your body will immediately be prepared for a possible major crisis.

In order to enable you to find out more about the potential crisis and to help you to decide just how important it is, there will be an immediate increase in the sensitivity of the sense organs. Your pupils will dilate and your retina will become more sensitive to light so that vision becomes more acute. Your hearing also becomes more sensitive. Animals prick up their ears, but in humans this reflex has long been lost. Your head will automatically turn towards the stimulus so that the best possible information can be obtained. Your muscles become tensed and your heart beat slows temporarily. You may feel it thumping away. Blood flow to your brain increases so that the best possible use of available brain tissue can be made and blood flow to the limbs diminishes so that if the limbs are injured little blood will be lost. You may feel cold and shudder. You will probably stop breathing for a moment or two. Any miscellaneous activities will be temporarily halted. If you're reading you will immediately lose your concentration.

The extent to which all these mechanisms are brought into action depends largely upon the size of the stimulus. If the stimulus is intense, surprising, unrecognized and entirely novel then the reaction will be most immediate and most extreme.

There is another immediate reaction which is not visible to the observer. The pituitary gland, deep inside the skull, produces a hormone which stimulates the adrenal glands. Unless the alarm is aborted and the stimulus recognized as harmless and unimportant the whole body will soon be affected by hormones produced in the adrenals. The respiratory rate will increase, the basal metabolic rate will increase and the heart rate and blood pressure will rise to help pump blood into the muscles at a faster rate.

## In case of emergency

Now imagine that instead of a cat having knocked the plate off and alarmed you the intruder had been an armed burglar. It is clear from his attitude that he intends to kill you as the only witness to his crime. You must escape. Information about the man is fed into your central nervous system from many sources; there is the information your eyes provide and the information your ears provide. At the first sound of the intruder the pituitary gland released hormones to put the body on a state of alert and now these hormones are beginning to help.

A hormone called the adrenocortiocotrophic hormone, for example, stimulates the adrenal gland to produce steroids and adrenalin. These hormones increase your blood pressure, close down your superficial blood vessels (making you pale) and improve the blood supply to the muscles. The shrinking of the surface blood vessels will ensure that if your body is superficially damaged you will lose relatively little blood while at the same time blood will be supplied to the essential organs such as the heart. Acid flows into the stomach to ensure that any food there is turned into sugar as soon as possible. The muscles are tensed ready for action. (A less useful reaction is the erection of the body hairs. When a cat is frightened its hairs stand on end, making it look larger and more fearsome to its opponents. When a human being is frightened his body hairs also stand on end. Unfortunately human body hairs are too short to be of any value. The reaction is automatic but of little practical use.) Clearly the body is protecting itself effectively for the changes which occur are likely to be largely beneficial. The body's owner will be able to defend himself more effectively thanks to these defence mechanisms. His ability to fight will have been heightened and he will be more prepared for flight.

The way in which your body responds to major stimuli can be divided into three parts. First, there is the alarm reaction when the adrenal glands are put on the alert, adrenalin is pumped into the bloodstream and the body prepares itself for action and may act. If the stimuli persist and are recognized as unimportant the body begins to adapt to them, the adrenal glands shut down and the body merely resists the stimuli, but does not respond to them. However, the adaptability of the human body has strictly finite limits. After a variable period of time, if the stimuli persist adaptation wanes and the body reacts again.

This mechanism of adaptation can be explained by using a simple example. If you sit in a room with a clock ticking your awareness of the ticking slowly fades. What has happened is that the receptors which pick up the impulse transmitted from your auditory apparatus becomes uninterested in the information. There is no action to be taken and so although the stimulus is there all the time the body does not take any notice of it. The clock's ticking has not stopped, but it is ignored. If however, the clock begins to tick a little louder then you become aware of it again. Indeed, if it stops you will also be aware that it has stopped. The stimulus will have changed and so the receptors will have to transmit this new information.

Although the body can adapt in this way, its ability to adapt is limited. A clock which ticks very loudly and persistently may be ignored for a little while but it will eventually force the fact of its presence into your consciousness. You will hear its ticking again. And once the body's adaptive mechanisms have failed, you will continue to be aware of that ticking. Eventually, you may find that the ticking becomes unbearable.

If the clock had been making rather more noise you might not have been able to ignore its ticking at all. The noise might well have been too loud and too insistent to pass unnoticed for even a short time. When this is the case the practical solution most of us would choose would simply involve moving the clock a little further away, underneath a cushion or into the next room. You might still be able to hear it but its ticking would perhaps be quiet enough to be ignored. If these choices had not been available you would have had to either accept the clock's ticking, leave, or go crazy.

In the lower animals a stimulus from the external environment is necessary before the system I have described can be activated. In human beings there is not necessarily a need for a stimulus from the outside world. The impulse can come from higher brain centres rather than the external environment. Such vague and introspective processes as thought and anticipation can alert the brain. Emotions themselves, of course, represent complex psychological and physiological responses to previously registered environmental changes for it is stimuli from the outside world which help us to feel love, hate, joy, fear and sorrow.

The human body cannot differentiate between situations. If you are faced with an armed burglar you must kill him, escape or be killed. If you lose your job you must look for another one. These are both stressful situations. The loss of a job which may have equally frightening effects as the confrontation with a burglar, will result in an identical physiological response. There will be the same change in the cardiovascular system, for example, and the blood pressure will rise in a similar way. The problem is, of course, that whereas the confrontation with the burglar will end fairly quickly with death or successful escape the state of unemployment and the associated fears may last indefinitely. Consequently the effects are also likely to persist and the unfortunate man without a job may have high blood pressure, a heart attack or a peptic ulcer as a lasting souvenir of his unhappy experiences. The unemployed man may want to find a job, he may actually look for a job, but he does not have complete control over his ability to find a job. And yet his body continues to help him cope, still under the impression that the crisis state is one which requires immediate action and unaware that its help is unwanted and indeed harmful. The blood pressure stays high, acid continues to pour into the stomach and the muscles stay tight and tense.

The human body is still designed for operation in environments where action must be taken quickly in response to stressful stimuli and where stimuli encountered are unlikely to persist. As the pace of life increases, however, so the number of impulses likely to incite a response from the body also increases. The seventies are said to be stressful not because stress-inducing events are by themselves any more traumatic than the events

213

of a century ago but simply because there are likely to be more of them, and because, there is likely to be less opportunity to escape from them. The continued and continuing physiological changes inspired by persistent problems result in damage being done to the extraordinarily resilient but nevertheless human organism.

Since it is not the problem itself which causes the stress-induced illness but the *victim's* response the effects clearly depend upon the victim's reactions which in turn depend upon his emotional makeup. Some people are better able to cope with distress. The effects which problems have depend upon the local circumstances and upon a great many different cultural and environmental factors. The well-fed businessman who encounters some minor problems may well suffer more than the victim of an aeroplane crash stranded in the desert. The summation and accumulation of pressures is also important. A man might shrug off a problem at work under normal circumstances but may suffer badly if he is already under a great deal of pressure at home.

Whatever stresses produce most trouble in your life I hope that this book has helped you avoid those which can be avoided and come to terms with those which cannot. In a full and rewarding life stress is often unavoidable, and even essential. The aim of this book is to show how you can protect yourself from its more harmful effects.

# Index

accidents, 117, 121
addiction, 60–3, 87, 118–19, 132
age as stress factor, 25–7
age structure of population, 14
aggressive behaviour, 15, 16, 27, 28, 31, 42, 90, 91, 117, 132
alcohol, 63, 80, 89, 118, 119–23, 158, 161, 171, 174, 196, 198, 205
alcoholism, 9, 119–23
allergies, 123–6, 154
amphetamines, 61
anorexia, 129–31, 192
anti biotics, 55, 136, 137, 149, 160, 161
anti depressants, 60, 174, 185
antihistamine, 125
arteriosclerosis, 168, 169
artery replacement, 165
asthma, 135–6, 154
automatic responses (physical defence mechanisms), 206–9

backache (lumbago), 137–8
baldness, 139–40
barbiturates, 61–3, 132
battered babies, 140–1, 183
bed wetting, 141–2
behaviour therapy, 58
benzodiazepines, 62–3, 132
beta blockers, 132
blood pressure, 12, 13, 58, 60, 91, 92, 96, 106, 112, 160, 162, 167–171, 176, 213

bowel disorders, 148
brain surgery, 58, 59, 132, 153
bronchitis, 7, 87, 136, 144
bureaucracy, 17–19, 22, 101, 102, 108

calorie control, 65–79
cancer, 7, 63, 87, 130, 191, 195–6
causes of stress: 4, 6, 7
  environmental pressures 4, 7–17
  personal pains, 25–31
  social strains, 17–25
city life, 7–9, 104–6, 163
cirrhosis of liver, 63, 119
colds and flu, 142–4, 149, 187
colitis, 80, 144–7
constipation, 145, 147–8, 151
cornerstones of life, 50–55
counterstress check list, 37
counterstress diet plan, 66–79
counterstress philosophy, 33, 34, 106–9, 204
crime, 13, 105, 121
cystitis, 148–9
  honeymoon cystitis, 149

defence mechanisms, 43–50, 124, 125, 181
depression, 10, 57, 58, 92, 105, 112, 128, 130, 132, 149–53, 170, 173, 180, 183, 184, 185, 192, 193; *also see* puerperal depression

dermatitis, 136, 146, 153–5
diabetes, 64, 144, 150, 155–7
diarrhoea, 145–7, 157, 158
diet, 65–80, 107, 112, 146, 147,
    155, 156, 157, 166, 168, 177,
    198, 205
diseases caused by stress, 24, 35,
    57, 90, 91, 111, 112, 114–16
drugs, 56, 60–3, 92, 118–19, 123,
    132, 133, 137, 138, 143, 146,
    147, 152, 159, 161, 164, 166,
    170, 173, 174, 176, 185, 186,
    189, 191, 193, 199, 205

elderly, the, 27, 130, 144
electrocardiography, 134, 135
electroconvulsive therapy (ECT),
    153
electronic brain stimulation, 59,
    60
epilepsy, 59, 158–9
ergotamine tartrate, 176, 177
exercise, 67, 68, 80–6, 89, 107,
    112, 165, 166, 167, 168, 173,
    189

family, 14, 24, 26, 50, 51
fits (epileptic), 158–9
flatulence, 80, 145
friendship, 50, 55, 105, 106, 193

gambling, 118–19
getting on with others, 42
glyceryl trinitrate, 128
grumbling appendix (mock), 146

habits, 43, 86, 89, 106, 163
hay fever, 136, 154
headaches, 12, 112, 122, 144,
    160–1
hearing loss, 11, 12
heart attacks and diseases, 5, 13,

22, 34, 80, 82, 84, 87, 109, 112,
    126–9, 135, 161–7, 179, 180,
    184, 191, 205, 213
heart, function, 162
heart – how to check, 83
heartbeat, irregular, 134–5
heart transplants, 165
high rise blues, 10, 11
hobbies, 36, 52–4, 106, 107, 165;
    also see leisure, sport
holidays, 54–5, 104, 105, 107, 109
hormones, 174, 175, 192, 194,
    195, 210, 211, 212
Houseman's disease, 171
housing, 10, 23
housewives' syndrome, 23
hydrocortisone creams, 155

impotence, 171–2, 180, 188, 189
indigestion 79, 80, 122, 130, 132,
    133, 151, 172, 179, 184
insomnia, 122, 123, 151, 172,
    173, 174, 179
insulin, 155–6
iron deficiency, 130
irritable colon syndrome, 79,
    146, 147, 158; also see colitis

jogging, 85–6

kaolin, 157

laxatives, 148
leisure, 52–5; also see hobbies,
    sport
Librium, 62, 92, 132
life style changes, 4, 90, 104, 106,
    108, 109, 193, 199
life styles, unusual, 90

mantra, 95
marriage, 4, 18, 19, 24, 26, 50, 51

mechanism of stress, 204–14
Medic Alert, 126, 159
medical help for stress diseases, 55–63
meditation, 91–2, 95, 171
meningitis, 161
menopause, 175
menstruation, 25, 150, 174–5, 194
Meprobamate, 63
messages to brain, 204–6
migraine, 136, 146, 154, 161, 175–7
Mogadon, 62
morphine, 62, 164
myocardial infarction, 162

nightmares, 176
Nobrium, 62
noise, 7, 11, 12, 13, 105, 163, 173, 212

obsessions, 177–9
obsolescence, planned, 9
Occupational Mortality Tables – extracts, 22, 167, 190, 193–4, 200
opting out, 104, 109
organization, 98, 99, 103, 107, 177
overcrowding, 13, 105
overweight, 162, 166, 177
overwork 112, 171, 179–80

palpitations, 180
penicillin allergy, 123, 126
pep pills, 61
permissive society, 25
personal relationships, 26, 41, 58
Peter principle, 21
pets, 54
phenobarbitone, 159
phobias, 57–8, 180–3
physical fitness, 53, 56, 64, 78, 79, 80–9, 107;
  how to test: 83–4
pneumonia, 191
population structure, 13–14
proofing the body against stress, 63–4
protest, 12–13, 102, 103
psoriasis, 183–4
psythotherapy, 57–8
psychotropic drugs, 92
puerperal depression, 184–5
pregnancy, 62–3, 182, 185
puberty, 25
pulse rate, 83, 95, 96

reactions, 210–13
relax, how to, 89–97, 107, 147, 179, 198
relaxation, 55, 89–97, 170, 171, 173, 176, 177, 179
religion, 24, 25, 54, 119
retirement, 4, 14, 18, 19, 27
rheumatic diseases, 185–7

St Vitus Dance (chorea), 187
sex, 25–6, 42, 51, 166, 171, 172, 174, 175, 180, 187–9
sinusitis, 160
Skylab experiments, 81
sleeping pills 60, 174, 182
slimming aids, 67
smoking, 63, 80, 86–9, 107, 112, 118, 119, 122, 134, 162, 166–7, 173, 176, 196, 198
  how to stop, 88–9
sphygmomanometer, 169, 170
sports, 30–1, 53, 68, 82–5, 166;
  also see hobbies, leisure
status, 9, 21, 27, 29, 30, 31, 42
steroids, 125, 126, 135, 136, 137, 184
stress-causing factors, how to identify, 36

217

stress threshold, 145, 154, 159, 160, 175, 184
stroke, 5, 22, 112, 167, 169, 189–190
stuttering, 190–1
suicide, 19, 22, 26, 41, 150, 152, 183, 191–4
symptoms of stress – index, 114–116

temporal arteritis, 161
tension, 91, 95, 96, 98, 112, 131–133, 160, 161, 174, 184
throwaway society, 100
thyroid disorders, 194
tranquillizers, 17, 23, 60, 171, 179, 185
tremor, 122, 132, 195
tumours, 161, 195

ulcerative colitis, 147
ulcers, 22, 130, 133, 180, 197–200, 213
underweight, 78

Valium, 60, 62, 92, 118, 132
vandalism, 8
virus hepatitis, 149, 150
vomiting, 197, 200, 201

warning signs of distress, 34, 35, 36, 126, 145, 146, 159, 160, 172, 175, 176, 178, 179, 184, 192, 193, 195
Weight/height table, 65
work, 19–22, 51, 52, 53, 106, 107

yoga, 90, 95